WILLOW SPOKES
AND
WICKERWORK

Willow Spokes
and
Wickerwork

*The Nature Book of Weaving
with Wild-growing Things*

by Cleo M. Stephens

STACKPOLE BOOKS

WILLOW SPOKES AND WICKERWORK

Copyright © 1975 by
Cleo M. Stephens

Published by
STACKPOLE BOOKS
Cameron and Kelker Streets
Harrisburg, Pa. 17105

Printed in U.S.A.

Library of Congress Cataloging in Publication Data

Stephens, Cleo.
  Willow spokes and wickerwork.

  1. Basket making. 2. Hand weaving. I. Title.
TT879.B3S73   746.4'1   74-11297
ISBN 0-8117-1900-6

Contents

Contents

Introduction

All down through the ages basketry has played a vital role in the culture of people throughout the world. Materials used for construction were of whatever the particular area had to offer, and the uses of the finished items were endless: sleeping mats, shelter walls, doors, hammocks, cradleboards, sails, fish traps, dip nets, creels, footwear, capes, skirts, belts, shields, helmets, armor, and household and storage utensils of every type, including baskets for cooking!

And the artistry of the basketry ran the gamut from the crude, quickly-made basket, designed for temporary uses, through the well-woven "work-horse" basket, and on through the works of esthetic art in which great pride was taken in the beauty of design and coloring.

It is impossible to estimate how long ago basketry made its appearance, for so perishable are the materials that only in dry, protected sites, such as certain caves, have they been preserved for the study of science. However, very old specimens have been discovered and dated. Some of the best preserved of these were found in dry caves of the western United States. At the excavations in Danger Cave in Utah, specimens of basketry were discovered that were proved by the Carbon 14 testing method to have

7

been made in 7000 B.C. And other parts of the world have yielded, from tombs of the ancients, a great variety of baskets. The best known of these tombs was probably that of Tut-ankh-amen, a king of ancient Egypt. This tomb yielded intricately constructed basketry made of esparto grass which was, and still is, a favorite weaving material of that area.

With archeology one of the author's many loves, she has been digging in cave excavations in the Midwest, and felt beneath her hands that unmistakable, cordlike texture of woven material. And always she could picture in her mind the dark-skinned hands that worked to form the intricate pattern that was now merely a few inches of scrap. Some of the pieces were identifiable as woven grass sandals, and others, heavier and much coarser, were believed to be parts of sleeping mats.

The uses of basketry have never lessened; on the contrary, they have increased steadily, with each generation utilizing the skills handed down from the one before, but adding its own creative talents to develop others. And the skill used to make the first crude basket, created when primitive man found the need for something in which to carry a hoard of nuts from one cave to another, developed, as increased ease of living afforded more leisure time, into the ability to create real works of art.

Each group of people brought to weaving the type of construction needed for their particular culture. The Hupa Indians, skilled craftsmen of California, made baskets so closely woven that they could hold water. Other tribes coated baskets with tar, clay, and other sealing substances, and used them for cooking by the simple method of dropping preheated rocks into the water and adding food.

Indians of the Northwest, known even today for their excellent weaving, put into their work a great sense of the esthetic, with intricate patterns in both design and color.

The beginning of basketweaving was, for early people, a matter of survival; and in some places it still is. But in areas that have gone modern, the old basketweaving skills have been put into practice as a commercial venture, with beautiful baskets, in intricate designs and colors, made and sold to tourists or shops. You can, for example, purchase a handsome basket, woven in the widely used coiled pattern by the Hopi Indians of the western United States; a huge conical storage basket, made by the natives of some African countries; or a tiny woven toy, no more than a fraction of an inch around. In Mexico you will find woven rackets for games, such as jai alai, and in India you will find the snake charmer with his cobra ensconced in a beautifully woven basket, complete with tight-fitting lid.

8

Introduction

The author has a tray made in Morocco that is of basketry woven tight as a drumhead; firm enough, in fact, to carry filled glasses without spilling. Other items in the author's collection are a handbag woven in the Philippines of banana bark and embroidered with plant fiber, a split white oak flower basket made in the Ozark Mountains, a coconut hat purchased in Hawaii, a small covered box woven in India, a legged basket made of raffia and reed, a wall plaque of reed which came from Hong Kong, a delicately woven cricket cage from Japan, and a bird cage flower arranger from Africa. And even with all these beauties, the author must be blindfolded and dragged past any basket shop she encounters.

Perhaps the writing of this book will dispel this hangup, for most of the items described and pictured here were made by the author or friends, and every phase of the work was a pleasurable experience.

Why learn the skill of weaving? Some day your very life might depend on it. On the other hand, weaving might merely furnish an opportunity to express your creative instincts. Granted, it is unlikely that you would ever need to master survival techniques in order to survive in the wilderness, but wouldn't it be reassuring to know that, if such an occasion should occur, you could? And from the other viewpoint, there is not a man, woman, or child alive who does not feel the urge to express his sense of beauty by creating some object of art peculiarly his own.

Isn't it true that basketweaving has always held a great fascination ever since you made your first crude basket from that "storebought" reed in Girl or Boy Scout crafts? And so it was with the author. But never has it enthralled her as it has since she began, several years ago, to experiment in weaving from the materials old Mom Nature so lavishly bestows upon us. There is that feeling of getting right down to the nitty-gritty fundamentals of our ancestors' ways of living, and the author has used these skills to good advantage on a number of occasions. She has landed her canoe on the beach of a wild island in the Gulf of Mexico and found a treasure trove of shells scattered on its sands—and found herself without a thing to collect them in! What to do? No problem. There in the woods grew that most beautiful of trees, a coconut palm, and in less than fifteen minutes we had two very creditable baskets and were gathering shells to our heart's content. Later, we discovered a Key lime tree on another island, and again a basket formed almost by magic, from a frond of scrub palmetto; we soon had it filled with the luscious little fruit.

The baskets just referred to are, of course, quickly made and crude, but the same pattern may be utilized to construct lovely, decorative items as

9

well. We collect materials where we find them and then weave them at leisure.

My husband, Ray, gets involved too, scouting through forest and swamp with me, cutting fronds, reeds, cattails. And we are certainly not alone in our interests; others, seeing the action, plunge into the projects with zest, first following our lead, and then creating new and attractive items of their own design.

Mostly our time for such projects comes in winter when Ray's construction business closes down. We hitch up our travel trailer and head south, presumably to hunt article and book material for me, but we always see to it that there is plenty of time to get into our many projects—fishing, shelling, weaving, etc. When we get all wrapped up in this weaving thing, the people of the trailer courts start gathering around and it soon becomes a community project, with the men getting into the act, providing materials, splitting fronds, and being generally helpful.

We hope you who try out our weaving methods will derive as much pleasure from them as we have.

CHAPTER 1

Patterns of Weaving

Though we are discussing primarily the weaving of basketry in this book, we cannot entirely leave out the weaving of tapestry and cloth, for the patterns of all three overlap. While basketry is generally of a coarse type of weaving, tapestry of a finer grade, and cloth weaving much closer and finer, many of the patterns and techniques are similar in all three types of weaving. As an example, the plaid pattern of a fine wool tartan can be duplicated in a lowly grass mat; and the rich colors and patterns of Navaho Indian rugs and blankets can be copied reasonably accurately with a mixture of grass, jute, and sisal.

So the crafts cross and mingle, and it is difficult to know where one begins and another leaves off. Maybe that is the fun of basketry—the challenge, the driving desire to experiment with more and more difficult projects. The challenge has been with humans since early man; and his ingenuity, through the centuries, and the artistic ability inherent to some extent in all of us, has caused him to develop the art of basketweaving in marvelous ways.

Through the past it was not always the highly sophisticated, cultured people who excelled in this art; nor was it a matter of the people of one tribe or area, or even of one nation, handing the skills on to another. On the contrary, identical patterns of weaving seem to have sprung from the grass roots, so to speak, all over the world. And while there are a few patterns and styles of weaving typical of certain areas, most of them are so similar as to be indistinguishable as to tribe or country.

However, the people of each area where basketweaving is practiced (and there are few where it is not) have certain patterns and styles in which they are masters. The Pomo Indians of California produce some of the world's most beautiful basketry, specializing in coiled and twined patterns of an amazingly fine quality.

Naturally the use the woven article is to be put to is important in determining its style of weaving; the basket that is to hold water or even small seeds and grain will, of course, be much finer woven than the fish trap that must be of an open and widely spaced design to fool the fish and allow a free flow of water through it. And the basket intended to hold only small, lightweight items need not be woven and reinforced in the sturdy manner of the burden basket.

But man was not only concerned with the prosaic; the esthetic entered into his basketweaving in a big way, and as he developed styles of weaving patterns his sense of beauty was at work and patterns in color began to take their place in basketry. Perhaps the sense of the beauty of colors sprang into being when a woman noted the purple stains on her basket left by berries she had lugged home to mix into the pemmican; or possibly a deep brown stain of black walnuts, toted in a burden basket, called to the attention of some dark-skinned man the fact that altering the color of his everyday equipment was a possibility. At any rate, such is the esthetic sense of humans, that from the birth of the first idea of dyeing to the present-day color sophistication, basketry patterns have taken on beauty in color as well as in weaving design.

Dyes and various methods of coloring basketry will be discussed in Chapter 15. This chapter is primarily concerned with styles and patterns of weaving. For this reason, and to convey ideas as clearly as possible, this chapter contains drawings of the various weaving patterns discussed throughout the book. The drawings are concentrated in this chapter so that an overall view may be had. Along with the drawings are brief written descriptions of each of these patterns. Complete, step-by-step directions for weaving the different articles are given in Chapters 3 through 13.

There are other styles of weaving we might have included here, but these are the basic ones; the others are generally modified versions of the basics.

Though certain patterns of weaving are worldwide, names for them differ, and in the following examples those titles are used which seem to most accurately describe the type of weaving.

We begin our patterns with the wickerwork (or willowwork). It is not necessarily the most important, though it is possibly the most widely used.

WICKERWORK (WILLOWWORK)

Wickerwork weaving is started with six crossing spokes. A weaver is then wrapped around the bunches of three, to anchor them. Now add one more spoke to make an uneven number (see Fig. 1-1).

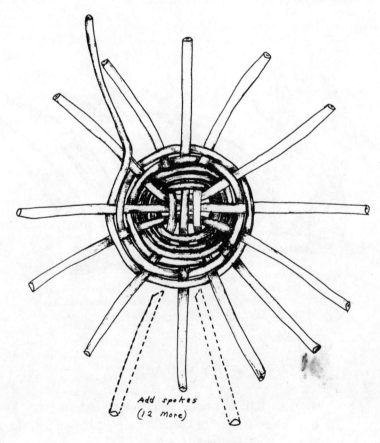

Add spokes
(12 more)

Fig. 1-1. *Wickerwork.*

Begin the over-and-under conventional weaving, forcing the spokes out to form a wagon wheel, and continue weaving.

As you work farther out, the weaving will begin to appear loose; to remedy this, more spokes will be needed. Insert twelve more spokes, pushing them into the pattern beside the others. (*Note:* In order to keep the number of spokes uneven, one spoke will not have a mate.)

Continue weaving, shaping the basket up as desired.

CROSS-WEAVING OF PALM FRONDS

The cross-weaving of a palm frond is a simple matter. Leave the fronds attached to the rib and start weaving by bending every other frond back and crossing it over the one next to it (see Fig. 1-2). Then weave the fronds on a diagonal slant, over and under alternately.

Fig. 1-2. Cross-weaving of a palm frond.

CHECKED WEAVING

This easy weaving pattern is usually made with flat material often of the same size (such as palm fronds or cattail blades). It is a simple matter of weaving over and under alternately (see Fig. 1-3).

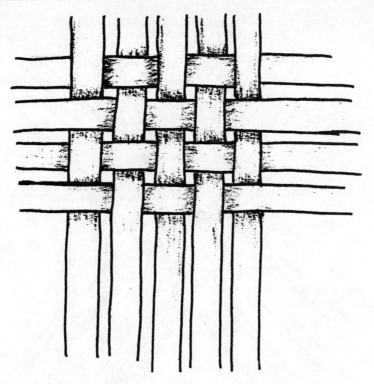

Fig. 1-3.   Checked weaving.

DIAGONAL BRAID

This braid may be made of any flat material, and may employ any width of material from whole fronds or cattail blades to narrow strips. The number of fronds determines the width of the braid, and any number can be used, always keeping in mind the fact that there must be an uneven number.

For the braid pictured in Figure 1-4, nine strips are used. Lay five strips on one side and four on the other and weave them across each other on a slant. When all have been woven in, fold the outside weaver on one side of the section of five forward and weave it over the four. Then fold the outside weaver on the other side forward and weave it to the center in the same way. Continue folding the outside weavers alternately and weaving them across. It is easy to make a long strip of braid by splicing a weaver just before it runs out. Insert a new weaver in with it and weave both of them for several spaces.

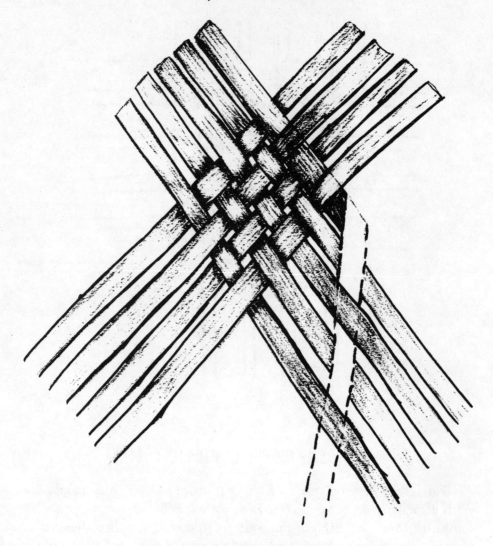

Fig. 1-4. *Diagonal braid.*

RING WEAVING

Lacy ring weaving can be done with reed or willow whips. It is usually used as single rows of "lace" between more substantial patterns of weaving.

A coil is formed and lashed to the row below with a pliable weaver. Then a second coil is formed, looping it into the first, and lashing it too into the row below, etc. (see Fig. 1-5).

16

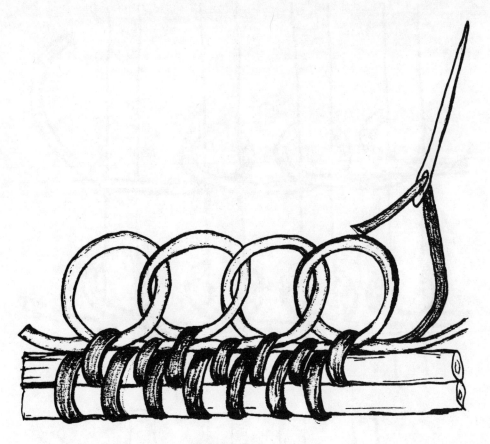

Fig. 1-5. Ring weaving.

WRAPPED WEAVING

Small, pliable weavers are wrapped around larger spokes (see Fig. 1-6), either in a loose, lacy manner or, for a more closely woven patten, bringing both the spokes and weavers closer together.

LATTICEWORK WEAVING

Round spokes are used here, wrapped together with softer, more pliable weavers. Wrap in front of the upright spokes and back of the horizontal ones, thus tying them together (see Fig. 1-7).

17

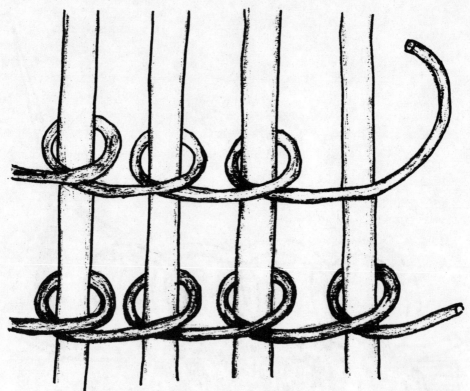

Fig. 1-6. *Wrapped weaving.*

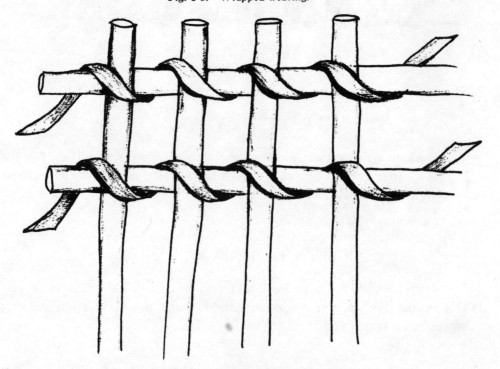

Fig. 1-7. *Latticework weaving.*

SIMPLE COIL

This pattern is made over a coiled base of one spoke, or several small ones, or a bundle of grass. Use a large needle for the weaver.

Curve the rod or spoke in a hoop and tie it. Then lash the hoop and the spoke together, as you go around the hoop with a soft, flat weaver, simply looping the weaver over the two (see Fig. 1-8). Other base material and weavers may be added as these are used up.

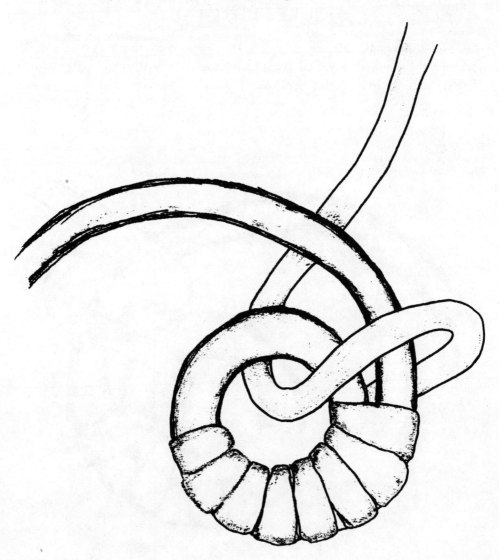

Fig. 1-8. Simple coil.

19

LAZY SQUAW COIL

This time-saving stitch is done in the same manner as that of the simple coil with the exception that it is given one or more turns around the spoke before looping it into the body of the weaving (see Fig. 1-9). It is a looser method than the simple coil.

FIGURE-EIGHT COIL

The same materials are used for this pattern as those in the simple coil, but the method is varied by looping the weaver into the pattern and around the spoke in a figure eight (see Fig. 1-10).

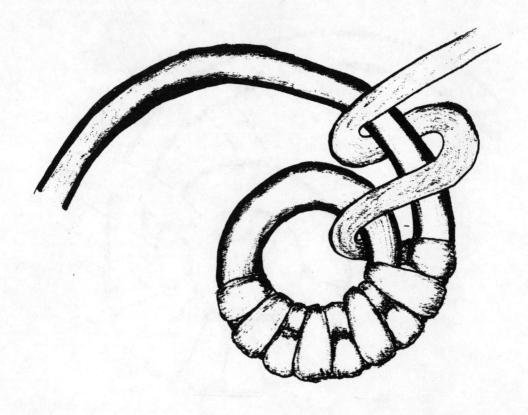

Fig. 1-9. *Lazy squaw coil.*

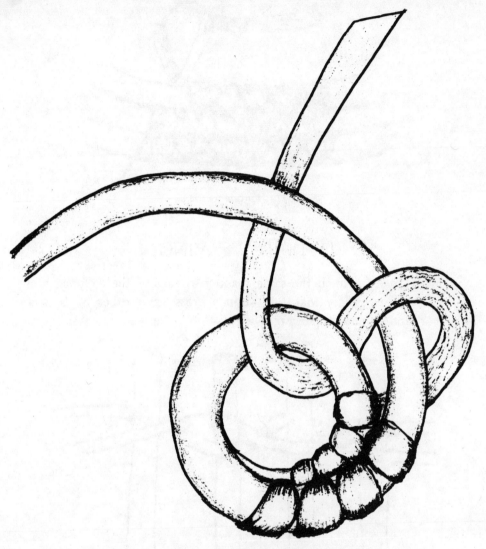

Fig. 1-10.   Figure-eight coil.

FURCATE STITCH

This too is a sewing pattern of weaving and requires a needle. For fine work, such as pine needle weaving, a darning needle will serve, but for larger materials a needle whittled from a piece of wood is excellent. This is a simple coil pattern with the exception that each stitch is caught into the middle of the one in the previous row (see Fig. 1-11).

Fig. 1-11. Furcate weaving.

TWINED WEAVING

This is done in much the same manner as that of the wrapped weaving, with the exception that two strands cross each other as they are brought around the spokes (see Fig. 1-12).

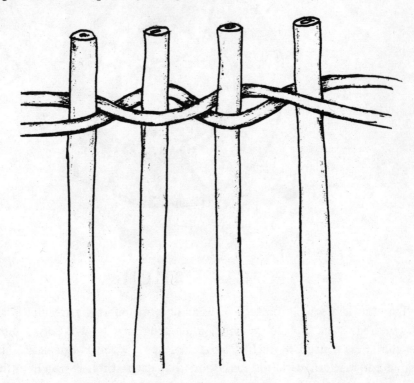

Fig. 1-12. Twined weaving.

22

CHAPTER 2

Materials and Their Preparation

Gathering materials from nature is half the fun of weaving, for it gives you a bona fide excuse for scouting in the outdoors. The area, of course, determines the type of material you will collect. In the southern United States there can be found tropical trees and plants ideally suited to the craft of weaving—coconut palms, Sabal palms, palmettos, bamboo, and the agave, or maguey plant, that yields ropelike sisal for both tying and weaving. In temperate zones, search out ponds and swampy areas where there are cattails, rushes, reeds, and grasses. Also hunt for creeks and rivers which have densely wooded banks, with trees festooned with the many kinds of vines which make excellent spokes and coil-weaving rods. It is here too that you will find the pliable willows. Northern zones, though not as prolific in the variety of weaving materials, furnish several that serve quite well. There are vines of several species, inner bark that may be stripped from trees, tough, tall grasses, etc.

Most basketry material may be used green and will eventually dry into tough, fibery stuff that lasts well, even with rough use. But there is a drawback in weaving green material, for it will shrink when it dries and you will find the weaving much looser than when it was first done. For this reason, it is often wiser to gather, cure out, and then dampen the material with water before weaving.

If materials are to be collected and stored for future use, it is well to observe some proven methods of curing. Not all types require the same curing method; so we will discuss them separately.

COCONUT PALM FRONDS

Palm fronds are a favorite material for weaving (especially large items), and we prefer to weave them freshly cut from the tree. They do not

Fig. 2-1. *The graceful coconut palm is probably the most useful of all trees, graciously offering to mankind not only its beauty but wood for shelters, thatch for roofs, nuts for food, and fronds for basketry and dozens of other uses. It can be found in most tropical and semitropical areas.*

shrink nearly as much when dry as other materials, but they will shrink to some extent and it is a good idea to make the weaving as tight as possible.

The most beautiful of the coconut weaving is done with the perfect fronds that come from the center of the tree, for these are not only more pliable but cure out an overall even color. Cutting a couple of these fronds from a palm does not hurt the tree.

Basketry woven from the fresh tree may be cured in one of several ways. If the item is not too large (hat or small basket), a good curing method is to place it immediately upon finishing in a food freezer (preferably overnight) and then set it out in the sun. There is something about this process (we can't explain it) that causes the basketry to turn a lovely even mahogany color. We cannot take credit for originating this method of curing; it is often done by professional weavers. We only know that it works beautifully. Of course, this process is not a strict necessity, for palm baskets, whatever the curing method, will turn out to be strong, sturdy items.

There are diverse opinions on curing methods. Some old-timers, who have been weaving from palms for many years, like to cure the fronds by laying them out on the grass to expose them to the sun by day and the moistening dew at night. However, our experience has proved that those cured in direct sunlight are more brittle; and they do not color up as evenly but are sometimes inclined toward brownish spotting. This especially holds true of fronds which have been taken from the more aged sections of palm trees.

One caution: if fronds are to be cured before weaving, separate them so that air can circulate freely among them. Otherwise they may mold and turn brown. Hang them in a shady spot or lay them out flat on a picnic table or another such spot.

Several of the styles of palm weaving described in this book, utilize the entire frond (complete with rib) or a half-frond (split down the middle rib, as in Fig. 3-2). But for other types of weaving, the fronds may be cut from the main rib, and in some designs, such as braids, split into even finer strips.

If dried fronds are used in this manner, they should be cut from the ribs several hours before they are to be used. Then, if even smaller strips are needed, ripping the fronds in strips from the lesser ribs of the branching fronds is easy if you insert a needle, pin, or the blade of a knife into them at the desired width and simply run it down the entire length, as in Figure 4-9. This is a speedy and efficient way of stripping.

With dried fronds, soak the material in water for five or ten minutes; then wrap it in a wet towel, paper, or leaves. This keeps it moist and pliable as you work. If you don't use all the material during the day, check to be sure it is not mildewing. In this case, though, it would be better to allow the fronds to dry and then repeat the wetting process when you are again ready to weave.

SABAL PALM FRONDS

These attractive palms, which grow prolifically in many tropical and semitropical forests, provide some of the finest weaving material to be

Fig. 2-2. *The Sabal, or cabbage palm, which grows wild in many tropical and semitropical forests, is almost as versatile a tree as the coconut palm. It too furnishes fronds for weaving and thatch and fiber for cordage; and the heart makes an excellent vegetable called palm heart or swamp cabbage, which can be eaten raw as a salad or cooked as cabbage.*

found. Tough and yet supple, their fronds can be used for a wide range of woven items. Probably the most important of these is the palmetto braid, used widely in the manufacture of hats, mats, and other articles sold commercially. The fronds are long and do not have to be spliced as often as some varieties, and the cured braid remains supple indefinitely.

The instructions for the curing and care of coconut palm fronds apply as well to those of the Sabal palm, with a few additional suggestions. We have observed that the coloring of these fronds can be controlled to some extent by the type of curing they receive. If they are cured in direct sunlight, they will turn a creamy white, though it seems that, as in the case of the coconut fronds, this makes them more brittle. When they are cured in a building, in the shade, the color is a pale green. An article patterned with the two colors is especially attractive.

These fronds will dye fairly well, though, as with all glossy type finishes, it is rather difficult to get them to take the dyes. For this reason it is better to use commercial cloth dyes, rather than those extracted from wild materials. A precaution: if several colors are to be presoaked for weaving, it is better not to wrap them together, for one color may stain a palm of another color.

PALMETTO FRONDS

Happily, this plant grows so prolifically that any landowner will permit its harvesting. It is a pretty plant, with its fan-shaped fronds but—let's face it—is a tough, pesky weed that tenaciously takes over woods and glades.

Weavers particularly like the texture of these fronds, for they are softer and finer than those of the coconut or Sabal palms, but they do have one fault: the fronds are not as long as those of the trees, which makes more splicing necessary. This is, of course, not a problem with small items, so it is a good idea to relegate the palmetto to these.

The same curing and soaking systems can be followed with the palmetto as with the coconut and Sabal. This material too, will dye, when dry, but better with packaged than natural dyes.

CATTAILS AND RUSHES

These tough plants may be found over a wide area and a wider range of climates than most any weaving material except the grasses. But you

Fig. 2-3. *The palmetto is a short plant, growing about two to six feet high. It can be easily identified, for it is made up of a bouquet of fans. This smaller plant can be used in almost all the same ways as the larger coconut and Sabal palms, especially in making some of the finest thatch. The fronds are narrower and shorter, and for weaving they are usually used for the smaller items.*

have to know where to look for them. They are invariably growing in the edge of water or on swampy land. In the midwestern and northern United States ponds are our favorite collecting spots; in the South, sloughs and swamps provide an ample supply. Here again, as with the palmettos, no one will object to the harvest, for they too are a pesky weed undesirable in a pond.

These, like the palms, may be woven immediately on collecting (though they will shrink, loosening the weaving), but they may also be cured.

Since it is more difficult to hang or spread these smaller blades to prevent them from molding, dry them in shallow piles, turning them occasionally during the curing process. And do pull the blades from the main stem to hasten curing.

These will dry a natural light beige, but may be dyed. Remember, when collecting these and other materials, to have plenty for your needs, for as they dry, they shrink to some extent, and you will have less material than you counted on.

Do not soak these blades too long before weaving. From 5 to 10 minutes is usually enough, especially if warm water is used.

These water plants, when properly cured and dampened, and in some cases when green, can be used for sewing with a large wooden needle, as in coil weaving.

Fig. 2-4. Cattails are widespread in all swampy localities and are quite versatile as weaving material. Strong and supple, they are good threaded into a wooden needle for the sewing of coil weaving, diagonal braid, and for dozens of other types of weaving.

WILLOW WHIPS AND VINES

Vines of all kinds grow everywhere, especially along the heavily-wooded banks of rivers and streams, and may be had for the gathering.

Willows too will be found along streams, and in moist lowlands. The weeping willow, with its long, drooping branches, is best for weaving, but since this is usually a treasured, cultivated garden tree, its branches may not be gracefully yielded up for harvesting. But as a second choice, the creek willow, especially the new sprouts that have sprung up from a cut-over area, is almost as good.

Fig. 2-5. Vines such as these make some of the strongest though not the most beautiful woven items. Often the entire length of the vine is knobby where the tendrils join, thus causing the weaving to be less uniform, as is that done with willow. But on the plus side, the vines are long, making splicing less of a problem.

30

The curing of willow whips is a moot question and we must admit that we have found no ready answer to the problem of getting them pliable after they have completely dried. For this reason, if the pattern demands that they be put through a lot of bending, we prefer to use them freshly cut, or at least no more than a day old. However, fresh willow whips, covered with wet grass or wrapped in wet paper, will keep their suppleness for several days.

Cut the willow whips, getting the longest and least tapering ones you can find. Run your hand down the length from the tip to the base to strip off the leaves. The whips are now ready for weaving.

Fig. 2-6. The willow tree, with its pliable long branches, is used for wickerwork and spokes for many kinds of basketry, including woven furniture. Items made of the willow are tough and durable. The weeping willow has the longest branches, but the sprouts of a cutover creek willow are almost as good.

31

REEDS AND GRASSES

The grasses are, of course, the easiest to collect of all the wild weaving materials, often requiring no greater effort than a pleasurable walk down a country lane.

By exercising your powers of observation, you can even find a variety of natural colors among them, especially in the fall as they mature and begin to dry.

The tall, thin, many-sided buckhorn stems, pictured in Figure 2-7, dry a lovely, glossy red-brown, and several of the field grasses have bright yellow or light red or orange stems. Strangely, you hardly notice these colors when looking at the growing plant, but after picking them, and

Fig. 2-7. *These are four of the kinds of grasses which make good weaving material. The grass on the left is buckhorn, which turns a glossy dark reddish brown when cured.*

32

Fig. 2-8. Grasses suitable for weaving are widespread in all countries of the world, and though all can be used in some manner for weaving, some, such as the tall, flat water grasses, are strong enough to be used with a needle for sewing in coil weaving. Some of the round-stemmed field grasses, in sheafs of from three to ten or more blades, serve well as rods for the coil that was, and still is, the most prevalent type of weaving among the American Indians.

laying them in bundles side by side, the variety of colors displayed is surprising.

The methods for preparing these grasses for weaving are simple. Cut and bundle them loosely, and lay them in a dry, shady spot for curing. Or you may use them while they are fresh. If they are dried, most of these grasses will last for weeks or months.

We can picture the delight of an Indian woman who comes upon a growth of tall grasses after traveling through an arid western desert. We can see her tying the bundles to the pack horse, or slinging them on her own back, anticipating the hours of weaving the much-needed household gear in the long winter to come.

With the wide variety and various textures of grasses available, it would be impossible to give detailed instructions for the preparation of each; but generally, some types of dried grass will become supple with a water bath of only five minutes, while others stay crisp in a bath of more than an hour. For this reason, the different grasses must be relegated to different kinds of weaving. Many flat grasses, for example, will be pliable enough to thread into a needle and use for sewing after five minutes soaking; while with some of the round-bladed kinds, no amount of soaking will make them supple to use in this way. This kind, though, can be used effectively as bundled rods for coil weaving.

The best plan to follow in the gathering of grasses, is to get a good supply of all kinds and then experiment in their uses.

SISAL

For the warp of loom-weaving, we have found that one of the best materials to be found in the wild is sisal. It is made from the agave plant.

To obtain the sisal, cut one of the big, glossy blades of agave, lay it on a smooth log, and pound it with a stick or rock until the pulpy outer covering is crushed, revealing the white inner fibers. Press or roll the pulp from the fiber. Then wash the fiber free of pulp and hang it up to dry.

At this point, the fiber can be combed with the fingers to separate it into threads. These threads will be of many lengths, some of them quite short, and for this reason it is necessary to twist several of them together. We could find no better way to do this than as the Indians did, rolling them with the palm of the hand over the thigh.

Now, with two of these fine cords of twisted fiber, you are ready to make a cord that will be closely twisted to form a good strong cordage. Tie the ends of the two to a tree limb or other object, and, stretching them out, start at the other ends to twist them together. When they are in a close twist, take hold of the middle of the strand, and, still holding the end out taut, fold it back, bringing all four ends together. Release the middle now and the four strands will twist together in a cord that will be quite strong.

PINE NEEDLES

Pine needles have been used for ages for the finest and most artistic of woven items. There are pine needles *and* pine needles, however. In other

Fig. 2-9. *The agave (or maguey or century plant) is one of the finest plants for cordage fibers to be found in the wilds. Its broad, thick blades are cut and thoroughly pounded to remove the outer pulp from the strong, white inner fibers. Strangely, there is a ready-made needle and thread in each blade of this plant. If you are in the wilderness and in need of sewing materials, just strip out the thorn, which grows on the tip of the blade, along with the fibers which are attached to it. Presto—a threaded needle!*

words, some are the good guys and some the bad guys as far as delicate, intricate pine needle weaving is concerned; for like humans, they come in long, short, fat, slim, stubborn, and cooperative varieties.

True, all types of pine needles *can* be used in weaving, but attempting to use the short needles of the slash pine or the nubby ones of the Australian pine can bring on a case of frustration and discouragement in short order.

Choose the longest, smoothest needles you can find. It seems that

Fig. 2-10. *Pine trees, such as this one, furnish long, supple needles for the weaving of the more delicate articles. There are many varieties of pines, and though they all can be used for weaving, those with the longer needles are best.*

many pines are constantly shedding their needles, and these can be gathered and stored in bundles until needed. Then soak a few at a time before weaving; five or ten minutes is usually sufficient. But conditions of weather and type of needles can play a part in this; so it is well to experiment and determine the length of soaking time that best meets the needs of your weaving.

WHITE OAK SPLINTS

Splint or split woven articles are the workhorses of basketry, for they are actually made of wood. Favorite trees for these splints vary with the weaver (hickory, white oak, etc.), but ours is the white oak, for the grain is usually long and uniform and splits out evenly. Of course, a damaged tree

Fig. 2-11. *The white oak, hickory, and other trees whose wood has the quality of splitting in long, uniform slices are used for split or splint basketry. They make the workhorses of the baskets: the old egg basket, laundry basket, bushel basket, etc.*

or one that has too many limbs growing from it along the lower trunk, will not work out as well as one that grows straight and without branching for a long distance up. A section at least five to six feet long and twelve inches or more in diameter is desirable but, of course, the longer the better.

With the log sawed out, square it up and saw boards from one to two inches thick. Both the squaring and the sawing of the boards can, of course, be done with a power saw, but we have seen skilled craftsmen wielding an old froe quite effectively for this purpose. Stand the block on end and force the froe through with blows from a mallet.

Now for the splitting of the splints or laths. The easiest way to do this is to rig a vise to hold the board firm; lacking this nicety, the board can be stood on end, or the end shoved into the ground and the board propped up against a log or tree at a slant. With the froe (or preferably a drawing knife) thin slats can be split out; the thinner and more uniform in thickness the better they will work out in weaving.

These may be woven immediately or, if they have been allowed to dry, may be soaked in warm water for several hours or steamed.

Check weaving is an excellent pattern for splints, but we have seen some nice baskets, made from splints in the wickerwork and other patterns. Almost any pattern suitable for bark weaving is also good for split wood. An example is the little square basket made of willow and slippery elm bark pictured in Figure 12-1.

TREE BARK

There are dozens of trees that will yield bark for basketry, but many of these (such as the paper mulberry and others from which such things as tapa cloth are made) are not available in most countries. For this reason (and because we want to feature the type of bark the least difficult to prepare) we are discussing primarily the weaving of willow and elm bark, with a bit about banana bark.

Even though there are many trees from which you can obtain weaving bark, the choice boils down to those which have the least number of twigs to interfere with the stripping out of long lengths. If there are many twigs, the stripping knife is stopped often, with breaks in the strips. However, in experiments, we did discover that it is possible to swerve slightly as the knife approaches the place where a twig grows and still retain the width of the strip.

If you are stripping bark from trees that are sturdy enough to stand firm as you work, you can strip from the tree without cutting it; but for smaller, more pliable sprouts, it is best to cut them and brace them on a slant by pressing the ends into the ground as you strip the bark, as in Figure 12-2.

The bark used must be from living trees, for the bark from dead ones stiffens. We avoid using any tree that will someday grow up to be one of the majestic giants we love so much, but by driving out on little country roads we find that there are plenty of crowded copses that will actually be benefited by thinning them out.

RAFFIA

It would be great if all weaving craftsmen could obtain the fine, soft raffia, that is made from the *Raphia pedunculata* palm, but unfortunately this palm does not grow widely. However, raffia can be found in almost all hobby shops, and if tying material and cordage is a problem, can be purchased.

For those reading this book who do live in the area of the *Raphia* palm, the following directions for preparation may be helpful. Cut the leaves of the palm after they are mature, but before they begin to curl, strip off the underparts and dry them. These thin, soft strips can then be split into whatever width you desire.

Raffia is the material most used in the sewing of coiled basketry such as the pine needle work described in Chapter 9, and it may be used for loom weaving, making a smooth, soft mat. This material is also one of the best for dyeing, taking the natural dyes derived from bark, leaves, berries, etc. almost as well as the commercial cloth dyes.

CHAPTER 3

Coconut Palm Fronds

The palm tree is probably the most versatile tree in the world. Its wood is used for buildings, its nuts for food, and its fronds for everything from thatch to cordage to basketry.

These fronds, ripped into various widths, can be used in most of the items depicted in this book. The uses are endless—basketry, shoes, raincapes, hats, walls of shelters, floor mats—you name it and the palm, with a little help from you, will make it. The possible patterns, too, are many and varied. Cross-weaving, check weaving, braid—all are possible with the palm.

But of them all, probably the most remarkable is the cross-weaving done by the Polynesians. It is a simple and speedy type of weaving. As a matter of fact, we have seen Polynesian men weave a large basket from splitting of frond to completion in exactly seventy seconds! The large basket, pictured in Figure 3-7, is done in this manner, as well as the wall hangings in Figure 3-10 and the hanging basket in Figure 3-9. The remarkable thing about this type of weaving is that the fronds themselves are ideally suited to it, without even removing them from the rib. The uni-

Fig. 3-1. Pretty girls, surrounded by a variety of coconut baskets, wear coconut hats trimmed with the immature buds of coconuts, which look like wood roses.

formly spaced manner in which the fronds grow on the rib suggests the pattern.

LARGE COCONUT BASKET

The large basket in Figure 3-7 is made from half of a frond. Here is how to make one like it.

Cut a pliable green frond from a coconut tree, choosing one on which all the smaller branching fronds are undamaged. With a knife, slit it down the middle rib, as in Figure 3-2. It will rip easily; but use caution to split the rib uniformly, for if there is a weak spot, the rib may break or bend in such a way as to distort the shape of the basket.

41

Fig. 3-2. Ray demonstrates splitting out a palm frond for the weaving of a large coconut basket.

Pull the half-frond around in a loop, the circumference determined by the size you plan to make the basket. Remember that for this type of weaving, unlike most, you will need an even number of branches. When you have decided on the circumference (using the middle section of the frond, where the branches are all of a like size), cut off the tip and heavy end of the frond and tie the hoop with sisal, or wire, as in Figure 3-3. Being somewhat purist in this back-to-nature bit, we think it is more fun to make your own sisal for tying and cordage by pounding out the fibers from the blades of an agave plant (see Chapter 2).

With the split rib at the top of the basket, begin weaving by the simple method of bending back every other frond in the opposite direction from that in which it naturally grows. Thus you will be crossing the branches over the ones next to them in pairs as you work around.

The second time around, give the fronds the old over-and-under conventional weaving treatment, as in Figure 3-5.

Continue weaving around, tightening the weaving as you near the

Fig. 3-3. *Here is how to form half a coconut frond into a hoop preparatory to weaving a large coconut basket as the Hawaiians do it.*

Fig. 3-4. *Sometimes a frond or two will split away from the rib, as in this photo of the beginning hoop for a large basket, but these fronds will weave in satisfactorily by simply holding them in place as you weave. Or new fronds can be spliced in by cutting the damaged ones back and splicing in new ones by weaving them in with the last few inches of the old.*

Fig. 3-5. The weaving begins by crossing every two fronds and weaving them over and under. Note that after the crossing, each frond will always slant the way it began.

bottom to cup it. A hint: holding the branches with clip clothespins prevents the weaving from loosening as you work.

Keep tightening the weaving until the bottom shapes in. When it is cupped, tie the branch ends into one or more bunches, as illustrated in Figure 3-6. These ends may then be woven back into the design or pulled to the inside of the basket through the openings and clipped.

Now for the finishing touches—and these may be varied, depending on the purpose for which the basket is desired. For the large basket in Figure 3-7, we added a trim on the rim made of strips of palm fronds which were wrapped around the exposed rib and in through the openings of the design. This adds to the strength of the basket besides making a neater rim finish.

For the handles of this basket, loop strips of frond into the top edges and securely tie the ends. Then wrap more frond strips around the entire handle.

The above basket is a basic design which may be varied in many ways. It may be a large, bushel-basket size, such as the one pictured here, or small enough to be used for a bun basket. For the small ones, use the fine tip-end of the frond. In this way, two baskets can be made from one frond half.

Not only may the size be varied, but the design can take several forms. For an especially strong basket, a coil-woven bottom may be laced in by

Fig. 3-6.   *This is one way to tie off a basket bottom. There are several ways in which this can be done. This basket is to sit flat; so the frond ends will be woven back into the pattern. For a hanging basket, the ends can be tied in a tassel.*

Fig. 3-7.   *A large finished basket. The rim is bound with fronds for added strength; and handles, made of several fronds, looped into the rim and bound with frond strips, are added.*

Fig. 3-8.   A large coconut basket can be made especially durable by adding a coconut coil-woven bottom. This bottom is bound in with the ends of the side fronds.

wrapping the frond ends into the edge of the coil weaving, lacing them in and out for several spaces, and then clipping them off.

One especially attractive basket, that may be woven in the same manner as that described above, is the hanging basket. For a nice trim on this one, tie the bottom frond ends in a tassel and leave it hanging. The handles are made by braiding two long strips from fronds (adding more strips as they are used up), crossing the braids, and looping the four ends into the top of the basket, as in the hanging basket shown in Figure 3-9. Fasten the handles securely by binding the lapping ends with frond strips.

You will note that the baskets in Figure 3-9 are in various stages of completion. The small one has been tied temporarily with twine, to hold it in the desired shape until it has cured out. However, this is seldom neces-

46

sary, for coconut fronds are extremely strong and durable and a basket made from green material is immediately ready for use, though the fronds will shrink to some extent. None of the baskets in Figure 3-9 have their rims wrapped with the strengthening trim. Though this is not necessary, it is desirable.

The baskets pictured in this chapter are only a few of the many that can be made of coconut fronds by this method of weaving. There are endless others, all of them attractive and practical additions to the family room, garden, or patio. Among them are a large deep basket to hold kindling beside a fireplace; a wide, shallow one for gathering flowers and vegetables; a large hanging basket to hold plastic swim toys near a pool; smaller hanging baskets to hold potted plants or artificial flowers, and others which can be used as decorations or for containers to cover flower pots.

Whatever their use, their creators take immense pride in baskets

Fig. 3-9. Shown here are three uncompleted palm frond baskets. The last step will be binding the rims with more fronds.

woven by this unique method, and they are also highly prized by friends lucky enough to have received one as a gift.

LARGE WALL HANGINGS

The decorative wall hangings in Figure 3-10 can be made quite large, five or six feet long, depending on the length of the palm frond. They may serve merely as decoration or, curved in to form a cup at the bottom, can hold a flower pot, garden tools, or swimming pool needs.

For such a hanging, cut a palm frond from a coconut tree, preferably one of the fresher ones from the middle of the tree.

Fig. 3-10.   Other examples of wall hangings vary in style.

To make the heart-shaped decoration at the top of the hanging, use about ten fronds. Starting at one side, begin weaving toward the heavy end of the rib by bending the tenth frond up and weaving it over and under the others to the top. Now weave the next one in the same manner, alternating the over-and-under process. Continue to weave until all ten of the fronds have been woven in as in Figure 3-11. Continue weaving until the pattern has cupped.

Now weave the other side the same way. Clip clothespins are good to hold the weaving as you work.

When both sides of the heart are woven, there will be a few inches of ends left. Pull these ends to the back and secure them there by tying them with sisal or twine (see Fig. 3-12).

Fig. 3-11. *The first step in weaving this large wall hanging is begun at the large end of the rib (though such hangings may also be begun at the small end). Bend a frond (in this case, the ninth frond down) back in the opposite direction from that in which it grows. Weave it to the top. Then, working up, weave in all the others in like manner. Now bend the ends over and continue weaving until all are woven back to the main rib. This forms the cup. Clip clothespins are a great aid to hold the work.*

Fig. 3-12. *Weave the other side in the same manner. The heart shape at the top is now complete. Pull the ends of the fronds to the rear and tie or tack them.*

Now begin weaving the body of the hanging. It is done in exactly the same manner as the heart shape at the top, but woven down instead of up (see Fig. 3-14).

After both sides have been woven, you have a choice of finishing the hanging to lie almost flat, or cupping it into a low, shallow cup as in the center hanging in Figure 3-10, or a deep cup like that of the hanging on the left in Figure 3-10. Regardless of the choice, it is finished off by weaving the remaining ends back into the body of the weaving (see Fig. 3-15).

The tip end of the frond was cut off before the final cupping of the hanging shown in Fig. 3-16 in order to give the hanging the wide flare at

Fig. 3-13.   This photo shows the completed heart.

Fig. 3-14.   The large lower section of the hanging is woven in the same manner as the decorative heart, only downward, beginning with the frond next to those used in the heart. Clip on some clothespins or tie the ends and weave the other side.

Fig. 3-15. Now finish the sides by continuing the weaving until they cup; then, curving them across each other, weave the ends back into the pattern. You may have a shallow or deep cup as desired.

the bottom. However, if a pointed one is desired, most of the tip, with its shorter fronds, can be left on.

The deep cup of the hanging on the left in Figure 3-10 was further strengthened and trimmed with a three-strand braid of palm strips, fastened around it. The top decoration of this one was cupped forward, lending the whole thing the look of an Indian cradleboard.

COCONUT HAT

There are several ways to weave a coconut hat. Some utilize the large rib in the edge of both the crown and brim; others have the small ribs retained and the large one removed, while in still others both the large and small ribs are removed. We prefer (after much experimenting) to use the large rib, shaved fine, in the inside circle of the brim, but removing all the smaller ribs in both the brim and crown. As a result, the hat is lighter in weight.

Fig. 3-16.   This completed hanging is about five feet tall.

The coconut hat in Figure 3-17 was woven in the cross-weave pattern, using only strips of ribless fronds for the crown.

For the crown, cut the fronds from the large rib. Then inserting a needle, pin, or small sharpened stick into the frond next to the small rib, rip the frond the entire length and remove the rib. It will take about twenty of these strips for the crown, but since there are two strips to each frond, only ten fronds will be needed. Of course palms do differ and the size determines the number of strips that will be needed, but as you proceed, the number needed will become apparent.

Now tie a piece of sisal or other cordage, or a strip of frond, into a circle about an inch and a half across. This is the form on which to start the

Fig. 3-17. This coconut hat is trimmed with undeveloped baby coconut buds, which look like wood roses and can be found under coconut trees after every high wind.

top of the crown. Bend the twenty ribless strips of frond in half and loop them through this circle, as in Figure 3-18.

Now for the cross-weaving. Begin crossing the strips, weaving them over and under, under and over, as in Figure 3-19. Check as you work to be certain that each row crosses alternately to the one before.

After you have woven a circle about six inches across, begin shaping the crown by weaving it over a wig form or head-sized bowl or by trying it on the head every few rows, tightening the weaving to fit. When it has the depth you want, cut the remaining ends off evenly to about three inches.

Now, bending an end under, weave it back into the body of the hat, making a finished point. Do this with every second frond. The remaining ends are reserved to lash the crown and brim together.

For the brim, split one of the long coconut leaves or fronds down the large middle rib, trimming the rib as narrow and evenly as possible, as in Figure 3-2.

Measure and cut a section of the frond of a size to fit around the

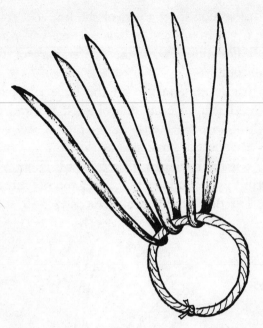

Fig. 3-18. *The coconut hat crown is built upon a hoop of cordage, with strips of frond from which the small ribs have been removed looped over it.*

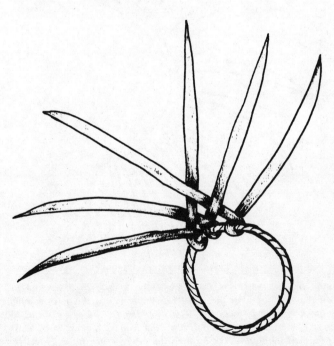

Fig. 3-19. *After the ring is filled with looped fronds, start cross-weaving, cupping after a few rows to fit the head.*

crown. Try to cut this section from a part of the leaf that contains fronds of a uniform size. Note that fronds at the base end are wider and those at the tip are quite small. For this reason, the center part of the leaf usually contains the most uniform fronds.

Now, leaving the fronds attached to the large rib, remove the small ribs by running a needle down each side of each rib and clipping it out, leaving two strips of frond attached to the large rib.

Tie the rib in a circle the same size as the crown. You will note that the frond strips are not thick enough for a close weaving; to make them so, cut more strips, derib them, and loop them over the rib between each of the other pairs of strips. This doubles the amount (see Fig. 3-20).

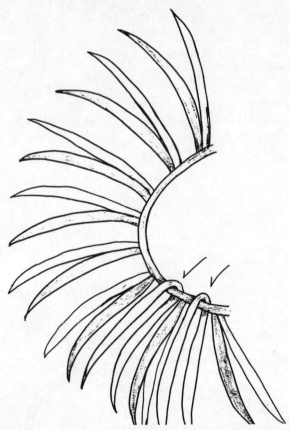

Fig. 3-20. *For the coconut hat brim, the larger frond is split to fit around the crown. The fronds are left on the rib, but with the small ribs removed, so as to form double fronds. To make the fronds thick enough for weaving, it is necessary to add more strips, looped between each of the pairs on the large rib. Cross-weave all the fronds, keeping the weaving flat for the brim. The hat is finished by binding the brim to the crown with the ends left from the crown. The final step is to finish the brim's edge in points by bending back each frond end and weaving it into the pattern.*

The weaving of the brim is done in the same cross pattern as that of the crown, but woven flat or slightly cupped. Lay it on a flat surface occasionally as you weave to be sure that it is not cupping too much.

When the desired brim width is reached, cut the ends of the strips to about 2½ inches, and bending them under, weave them back on a slant into the body of the brim. This makes a pleasing pointy trim on the edge.

The brim and crown are now ready to be joined. Lash the two together by looping the frond ends, that have been left on the crown, over the rib of the brim between the strips on it, several spaces back. These ends will lap over each other and will be anchored firmly.

The hat is now ready to be used as is, or trimmed. A woven grass band is attractive. It may be made in the same manner as the headband in Figure 8-4. Or, as we have done in this hat, trim it with coconut "wood roses." These are the undeveloped buds, the baby coconuts, which can often be found under the trees after a strong wind has dislodged them.

SHELTER (OR CHICKEE) WITH WOVEN WALLS

One of the most quickly constructed shelters is a thatched lean-to, such as the one in Figure 3-21. It consists of four upright poles, sunk in the ground, four more poles, to form the eaves, and eight poles for beams tied across the top as a roof support for the thatch. If the shelter is to be more permanent, it would be wise to tie on another eight poles across these to form a mesh, which holds the thatch more securely.

The chickee frame in Figure 3-22 is about eight by ten feet by six feet high, but for an overnight shelter could be much smaller. Also, in deep woods, the location could be chosen so that the uprights could be living trees.

When we made the chickee in Figure 3-21, we were in a tropical area where coconut palm fronds were available. Though these are not the best of thatch, they served our purpose for we wanted the shelter primarily for shade and not as protection from rain. There are other thatch palms with more solid leaves which will go on almost in the manner of shingles, lapping the rows from bottom to top, and making the roof waterproof. However, Sabal palm, palmetto, pine boughs, cane, or almost any leafy twigs will serve if enough are used, and tied on securely. This holds true for the woven walls also, for, though we have pictured only two types of weaving and materials, dozens of others can be used, depending on the material at hand.

Fig. 3-21.   *This shelter, or chickee, is made of poles and coconut fronds. Since our need was only for shade, we thatched this one with coconut fronds; but there are other palms which serve better for a weatherproof roof. Palmettos, though smaller, when installed like shingles, with an overlapping pattern, are better to turn rain.*

Fig. 3-22.   *Ray ties off the pole framework for the shelter.*

One of the wall panels of the chickee pictured in Figure 8-6 is made of one coconut frond, woven from the rib; the other is of sisal and tall grasses, woven on a crude loom constructed from tree limbs. These are described immediately below under Coconut Frond Wall Panel and in Chapter 8 under Grass Wall Panel.

Coconut Frond Wall Panel

This wall section is made of one coconut palm leaf, woven from the rib. The weaving is the same as that done to make the large palm frond basket in Figure 3-7.

Fig. 3-23. *The weaving of a wall panel is done in the same cross-weaving as the large basket pictured in Figure 3-7.*

Cut a limb from the fresh, undamaged section of a coconut tree; the older fronds are inclined to be brittle, and though they would work, if fresher ones were not obtainable, they would not, of course, be as attractive.

The weaving is done by crossing every two fronds, and for the entire weaving thereafter, those fronds will always slant in the direction in which they are started, as in Figure 2-24. The only thing conventional about this weaving is that this too uses the over-and-under pattern, once the fronds are crossed, but it is done on the diagonal. Continue weaving alternately over and under. If clip clothespins are available, use them to hold the weaving as you work.

Fig. 3-24. *With one side of the wall panel finished, the other is started.*

When a side is finished, fold back the end fronds and weave them from the rib out, as in Figure 3-25.

Binding or lashing the sides of the panel is the next step. Cut two slender, uniformly sized limbs the length of the height of the sides of the panel, and, bending the ends of the fronds over them, bind them to the sticks from top to bottom with sisal, twine, or more of the fronds cut from another leaf, in a cross binding as in Figure 3-26.

When both sides are bound, the wall panel is ready to tie to the eaves and to the upright poles of the chickee. A panel of this type, made from a large palm leaf, forms a wall section about a yard wide. If it is to be made more waterproof, more fronds, cut from another leaf, can be woven through the rather open section near the rib. However, if this is to be merely a shelter to offer shade from the sun, the pattern is so attractive that it should be left as is.

Fig. 3-25. *The frond ends at the edges of the wall panel are looped back to form a square end.*

Fig. 3-26.   *The sides of the wall panel are lashed in over a pole or sapling the height of the chickee wall.*

CHAPTER 4

Sabal Palm Fronds

The Sabal palm (or cabbage palm) furnishes some of the finest material possible for weaving. For many generations it has been used commercially for weaving hats, mats, and dozens of other items for sale in shops, and has even been a lucrative crop for families in the South, who harvested it and sold it to weavers.

Records of its use go back hundreds of years, but if the truth were known, that might turn out to be thousands, for, with this great material there for the taking, early man was certain to have used it.

Especially is it excellent to use in diagonal weave braid, but almost anything that can be made from coconut palm fronds can also be made from the fronds of the Sabal—but not on such a grand scale, for the fronds do not grow in the long drooping form of that of the coconut palm, but in more of a cupped fan shape.

However, this fan shape lends itself to some unique patterns of weaving altogether different from those that can be created with other materials. The basket made of two Sabal fronds and the wall fount are examples. Instructions for making and photos of these are to be found in the following pages.

63

WALL FOUNT

This wall urn or fount is made in the same weaving pattern as the large wall hanging in Figure 3-16, but instead of using coconut palm fronds, the Sabal palm was used.

The small, short fronds on the stem end are first removed, and then the weaving proceeds as in the large wall hanging.

Fig. 4-1. *The woven wall urn (or fount) was made in a diagonal braid pattern of strips of Sabal (cabbage palm), and trimmed with a coconut wood rose.*

Fig. 4-2.   This is the beginning of the wall urn.

BASKET WOVEN FROM TWO LEAVES

To make this basket (Fig. 4-3), cut two of the freshest fans from the Sabal palm tree. Cut off the stems of the fans to within about three inches of the fronds; then cut out the curved-up center fronds so that the fans will lie flat.

Now tie the fronds together, in the position shown in Figure 4-4. The fronds willl serve as the spokes for the twined weaving. They are pulled out to form an oval as the weaving is done (see Fig. 4-5).

For weavers you can use any thin, pliable material such as vines and willow or other long slim branches. Palm fronds may be used, as well, but these are soft and the basket will not be as firm as it would be with the

65

Fig. 4-3. *Two Sabal palm leaves were used to make this basket.*

Fig. 4-4. *The two leaves of the Sabal palm are tied together in the position shown.*

woody whips. For the basket pictured here, we used small vines, woven in the twined weaving pattern, as in Figure 1-12.

This is a simple style of weaving that may be made with the weavers either widely spaced or close together, depending on what the basket is to be used for. The technique of twined weaving is slightly different from that of others, as you are working with two weavers, with one passing over and the other under the spokes at the same time.

When the bottom of the basket is as wide as you want it, start shaping the fronds up to form the sides. Continue weaving until about four or five inches of the top fronds remain.

The rim can be finished off in one of several ways, but since this basket is not as firm as some other types, we like to reinforce the rim with a hoop made of a tree branch.

Loop the branch in a hoop the size of the top of the basket and tie it in several places to the rim. Now begin wrapping the ends of the fronds around the hoop and down into the weaving. With each frond wrapping over the one next to it for some distance, the fronds are securely lashed in. An even stronger rim can be made by using a long coconut frond and wrapping it on top of the others.

Fig. 4-5. *The weaving is done with long strips of frond or vine in the twined pattern, as illustrated in Fig. 1-12.*

67

Fig. 4-6.   The rim is a hooped tree limb bound with the ends of the fronds.

A handle, or pair of handles, can now be added, by looping fronds into the weaving and binding them as in Figure 4-7.

BRAID HAT

This lacy hat is easily made, for it is simply composed of long strips of braid, sewn together. However, it can be quite time-consuming; a lot of braid is needed. But faint heart ne'er won pretty hat, and anyway, the braid can be woven while you watch TV.

The amount of braid needed for the hat depends on the width of the braid and the width of the hat brim. The wise plan is to make up a long strip (being sure before you start to have an ample supply of material) and begin forming the hat. You will soon be able to determine the amount needed; if you find there is not enough, weave some more and then go on with the hat.

The hat with the very wide brim, in Figure 4-8, takes between six and seven yards of one-inch-wide braid. This braid was woven of strips of Sabal between ⅛ and ¼ inch wide.

Fig. 4-7. *This small basket, which is three years old, is proof of the durability of palm frond weaving.*

Fig. 4-8. *For this braid hat, weave a long strip of braid, in either the lace-edged pattern or the plain, of strips of Sabal palm fronds. This hat is trimmed with shells and green-dyed raffia, but is quite attractive plain.*

The strips were ripped out by inserting a pin or needle in a frond, as in Figure 4-9, and pulling it down the entire length. Begin at the rib, ripping the two halves of the blade from it, and then, measuring the width needed for the strips, rip them from the halves.

How to Make Lace-Edged Braid

Plain diagonal braid, as in Figure 4-11, is fine for hats, but the lace-edged type has an airy, open quality that makes it especially attractive for this purpose, and it is almost as simple to make as the plain pattern, once you get the hang of it. The instructions look complicated at first glance, but by following them step by step and watching the photo, the method soon becomes clear.

Use strips of Sabal palm (or any other flat blade) ripped about ⅛ inch wide. The lace-edged braid is woven very much like that of the plain pat-

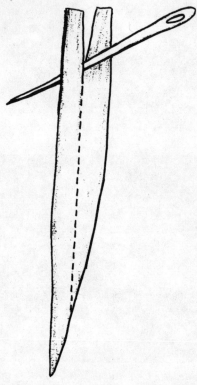

Fig. 4-9. *To split out the strips of frond, use a needle, pin, or knifeblade and simply rip them the desired size. For a fine braid they may be as narrow as ⅛ inch.*

70

Fig. 4-10. To weave a plain braid, begin by crossing the strips and weaving them in the over and under method.

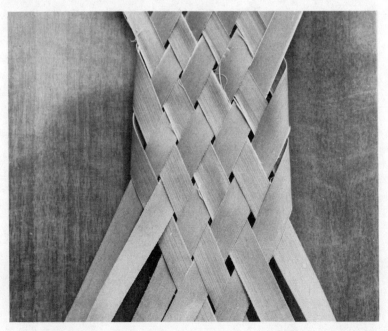

Fig. 4-11. After all the fronds are woven across, turn the outside fronds over and weave back to the center, alternating from one side to the other.

tern, with the exception that there are only three strips on one side of the crossed groups and six on the other. A larger or smaller number of strips can be used, making the braid wider or narrower, but we like the nine-strip braid, for it seems just right to curve on the bias for the crown, without being so small as to be tedious to work with. A large braid, made of wider strips would naturally make a coarser-looking hat. Of course, if you are out in the open and in a hurry for shade, the large braid would work up much faster.

When you begin weaving the braid, remember that you will be weaving *from* you. The author flubbed completely when she first tried to make this braid from written instructions only, for she was weaving toward herself and all the lefts and rights were wrong!

Place the groups of strips on a table or other flat surface, with the three strips on the right side, slanting over the group of six. Working from

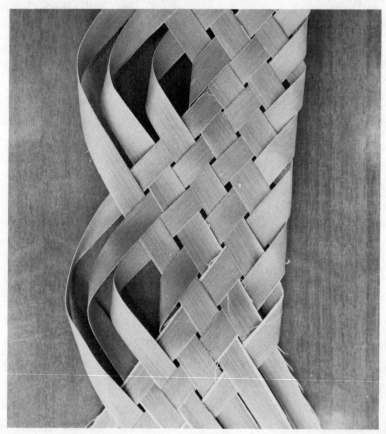

Fig. 4-12. *To weave a lace-edged braid, loose loops, increasingly larger, are woven at one side.*

72

you, weave the inside strip of the three over the inside one in the group of six, and then under and over, crossing all six.

Weave the second of the three under and over to the other side, making sure that it crosses the six in a manner just opposite to the one above it. In other words, if the one above went over, the next must go under.

Now weave the third strip over and under to the other side.

Now you have six strips pointing left and three right. You are now ready to begin to weave the main part of the braid.

Turn under the fourth strip from the left and weave it under one and over one.

Now weave the outside right strip over and under to the center.

For the first scallop, curve the third strip on the left into an arc, with the underside on top. Weave it over one, under one, and over one to the center.

Bend the right outer strip forward and weave it over, under, and over to the center.

Now curve strip number two, on the left, forward, and with the underside on top, make the second scallop, a little larger than the first, and weave it to the center.

Bend the outer right side strip forward and weave it to the center.

Curve the outside strip on the left into an arc for the third scallop, and making it still a little larger than the one before, weave it to the center (see Fig. 4-12). This completes the pattern of three scallops.

Repeat the process, weaving the fourth strip on the left for the next scallop, and continue until you have the length braid needed.

You now have a combination of plain braid edged by scallops. This can be used throughout the hat by sewing it with the scallops lapping over the next strip of braid, or it may be used only as an edging, as one would use lace.

When a strip is almost used up, it is easy to splice in another one by simply weaving it in with the last couple of inches of the old one.

Forming the Hat

After a long strip of braid is woven, begin the crown of the hat by curving the end of the braid into a tight circle and sewing it with sisal or

Fig. 4-13. The braid is sewn with sisal or thread in coils. Shape to form the crown as you sew; then continue sewing on down, forming the brim by fulling the edge as you sew.

thread. The circle will not be perfect, but the braid is surprisingly stretchy and easily shaped, for the type of weaving makes it lay on the bias.

Continue coiling the braid around and stitching it to the edge of the row before.

There are two ways to shape the crown; one is by working over a head-sized bowl or wig form, and the other is simply by guess-sewing a few rows and trying it on for size as you work.

When the crown is deep enough, place it on a flat surface and begin the brim by continuing to sew on braid, stretching it on the outside so that it will lie flat.

The hat in Figure 4-8 was trimmed with small, drilled rosecup shell and embroidery of dyed raffia around the crown.

CHAPTER 5

Palmetto Fronds

Though much smaller than the leaves of the coconut and Sabal palms, those of the palmetto have a softness and flexibility that make them an excellent weaving material. Add to this the fact that it is an undesirable weed and you have a good, easy-to-obtain source of material.

Because of the shorter fronds, this plant can be used to better advantage in the making of smaller items such as fans, small baskets, etc.

Since palmettos can be used in making most of the items made from the leaves of Sabal palms described in Chapter 4, there is no point in going into details on individual articles. However, we thought the quickly made palmetto fan and the fly swatter deserved mention. A short write-up on the fan will serve. The fly swatter is so simple it needs no directions.

FAN

To weave a fan from one palmetto leaf, first remove the very short fronds near the stem end; then rip the fronds apart down to the rib.

Fig. 5-1.   *This fan is made of palmetto.*

Now, beginning in the center, lap the two center fronds and begin the diagonal weaving as described in Chapter 1 on weaving patterns (see Fig. 1-4). The thing to remember about this unusual pattern of weaving is that every row begins with the crossing of two fronds, and each frond, once woven in, always turns in the same direction (see Fig. 5-2).

When the weaving is finished, the ends of the fronds are turned under and woven back into the pattern.

Fig. 5-2.   *Weave the palmetto fan from the stem and then weave the ends back into the pattern.*

Fig. 5-3.   *A fly swatter is simple when woven in the diagonal pattern. The ends are bent over and woven back in at the top, and at the base, are gathered into a bunch and bound onto a handle. The handle is then lashed to the swatter.*

CHAPTER 6

Cattails and Rushes

These are excellent material for many types of weaving. It was, in fact, used, often in combination with other materials, in a number of the wide variety of articles pictured in this book: hammock, mats, burden basket, shoulder bag, sandals, coil basket, etc.

For weaving with dried cattails, soak them for five or ten minutes in warm water in a bathtub or the sun-warmed shallows of a stream or lake, or use freshly cut. But remember that freshly cut materials of almost any type will shrink, and must be woven quite closely to compensate.

For some types of weaving, the stiff end of the cattail blade can be used as a needle or weaving sword, or an awl can be applied to open holes, or the blade can be threaded into a large wooden needle.

All of these methods were used in making the items pictured in the following pages.

Fig. 6-1. Most of these articles were woven partially or entirely of cattails, and in many different patterns.

SANDALS

In cave excavations of living sites of early man, one often uncovers pieces of mat material recognizable as parts of woven grass sandals, and occasionally an entire sandal is recovered. These are usually woven in the coil pattern such as those in Figure 6-2. As in styles of shoes today, the ancients had their own preferences, for some of these are simple scuffs and others complete shoes.

To make the scuff, pictured in the center of Figure 6-2, begin with a coil or rod made of about ten blades of grass (depending on the size of grass). To hold the grass together, tie it in two or three places with a bit of sisal or thread.

79

Fig. 6-2. Three varieties of sandals, made from cattails over a rod of grass, and from corn shucks.

Now thread a large darning needle (or wooden needle) with a weaver of cattail blade. Any flat plant can be used for this purpose; a strip of palm frond, with the rib removed, works quite well.

Bend the rod of grass up (about seven inches for a size 7 shoe) and tuck the weaver end into the bend, as in Figure 6-3.

Begin looping the weaver in a figure eight over the two rods of grass and continue on up until the two are woven together.

Bend the rod down and with the needle, continue the figure-eight stitch, tying the third row of rod into the other weaving, as in Figure 6-4.

Curving the grass rod as you reach the end of each row, continue to weave it in, until you have six rows, three on each side of the center groove. As the grass blades run out, keep adding more to the rod to keep it a uniform size.

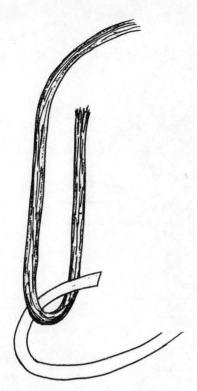
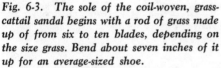

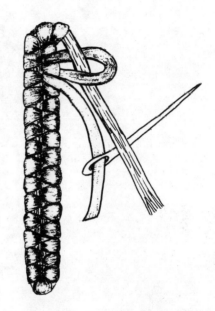

Fig. 6-3. *The sole of the coil-woven, grass-cattail sandal begins with a rod of grass made up of from six to ten blades, depending on the size grass. Bend about seven inches of it up for an average-sized shoe.*

Fig. 6-4. *Thread a wooden or large darning needle with a damp strip of cattail and lash the rod together in a figure-eight stitch, as described in Chapter 1 on weaving patterns; keep turning the rod as you reach the ends.*

At this point it is necessary to enlarge the sandal for the wide part of the foot. This is done by bending the grass rod back about a third of the way from the toe as in Figure 6-5, and weaving it in. Bend it again when you reach the same spot on the other side of the sandal.

Now for the finish of the sole. For the final row, continue weaving the rod in all the way around, as in Figure 6-5 (the new row is designated by a broken line).

The sandal or scuff uppers can be made in one of several ways. The sandal pictured in Figure 6-6 has both a heel and open toe, but the simplest to make is the scuff shown in the center of Figure 6-2 which is held on only by the band across the foot. The band is of check weave of a flat material (cattails, in this one), with the strips looped across the scuff and into the sides of the sole. Tuck in another flat strip and weave it back and forth across, as in Figure 6-7, until the other side is reached.

81

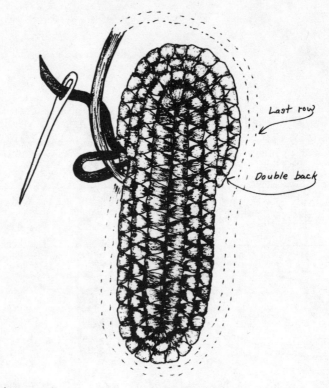

Fig. 6-5. *Continue weaving around the sole until there are six rows (three on a side); then double back to broaden at the toe. Turn again at the same place on the other side of the sole and then continue all the way around. This finishes the sole.*

Fig. 6-6. *A sandal may be a scuff or complete with heel and side straps.*

Fig. 6-7. *To make the top of a scuff, loop four or more cattail strips in through the sole near the edge and over the foot; then weave another blade across these, filling in to the other side.*

The scuffs may be left plain or trimmed with raffia, dyed grass, or cattail embroidery, with small shell "flowers." The shells used in the little sandal in Figure 6-1 were rosecups, with a hole drilled in them, in order to hold them on. For the shells, you can use any cupped shells found on the beach. You can also buy them in several sizes from shell shops.

LARGE SHALLOW BASKET

This basket is made in the figure-eight coil weaving pictured in Figure 1-10. Though this one is made of cattails, palm fronds or a wide-bladed grass will work as well.

It is best to let the cattails cure for at least twenty-four hours, and then before using them soak them in warm water for about five minutes. If the material is too fresh or too wet, it will shrink badly when the basket is aged and the weaving will be too loose.

The variegated pattern in the basket shown in Figure 6-8 is created by using the entire length of the cattail blades, as each blade is a deep green in the upper part and a creamy white down near the base. The rod is willow.

In using material such as manufactured pulp reed purchased from hobby shops, which comes in long rods exactly the same diameter throughout the entire length, there is no problem with keeping the diameter of the rod uniform, but with the tapering limbs of willows, which have been used in this basket, it is necessary to improvise. For this reason, start the coil with the large end of a single willow whip (see Fig. 6-9), and then, as the weaving advances to where the rod tapers, add two more whips, trying to

Fig. 6-8.   *This large flat basket is made of cattails woven over a coil of willow whips in the figure-eight pattern.*

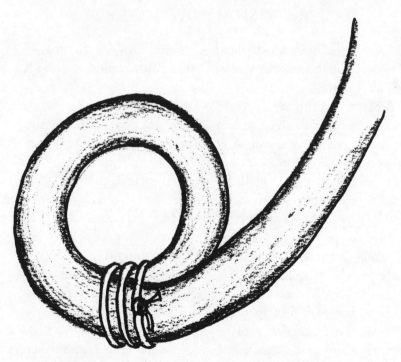

Fig. 6-9.   *The basket is begun with a coiled willow whip.*

keep the circumference about the same as that of the large end. This can be accomplished by adding the small sections of the new whips in the sections where the medium circumference of the old whip occurs.

For the stitching, thread a cattail blade in a large needle (we prefer a needle whittled from a piece of hardwood) and use the figure-eight stitch (see Fig. 6-10).

As the rows grow larger around, it is necessary to add stitches. For the first four rows, after the first coil is formed, add an extra stitch after every third stitch of those in the row before. For the next four rows, add an extra stitch for every fifth, and for the next four rows, an additional one to every seventh, decreasing the number added in order to keep the bottom of the basket flat.

The above rule is not infallible, for of course the width of the cattail blades determines, to some extent, how many stitches should be added. The best plan is to use the figures above as a guide but lay the basket down on a flat surface occasionally, to determine that it is not cupping, and then decrease or add numbers of stitches accordingly.

Continue weaving in this manner until the bottom of the basket is the size you desire (the bottom of the basket pictured in Figure 6-8 is 15 inches across).

Fig. 6-10. *A cattail strip is threaded into a wooden needle and looped around the coiled willow with the figure-eight stitch.*

At this point, shape up the sides of the basket by adding fewer stitches. If the sides are to come up abruptly, don't add any stitches, but if you want them to slope, add only an occasional stitch (about one in every ten), checking the shape after every row to decide that it is sloping as desired.

As a cattail weaver runs out, splice in another by simply weaving a new one in with the last three inches of the old one.

The handle of the basket in Figure 6-8 was made of cattail blades by looping two long blades into the open weaving of the rim and lashing them together with a figure-eight stitch of more cattails (see Fig. 6-11), catching the ends in at the same time.

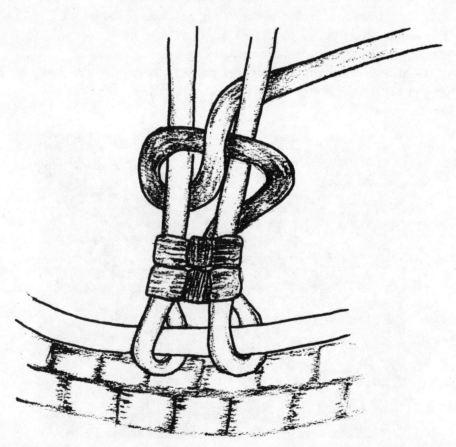

Fig. 6-11. *The basket handle is made by looping two cattail blades around the rim and binding them with loopings of cattail strips.*

Fig. 6-12.   *A section of the handle, close up.*

Fig. 6-13.   *The two sections of the handle are formed into one.*

HAMMOCK

For the woven hammock in Figure 6-14, we used sisal for the warp, because of its strength; jute for the bird design, because we happened to have several strands already dyed; and cattails for weft, because it was late summer and they were long, strong, and available. But of course palm fronds, grass, or willows could just as readily be used in place of one or more of the above.

Before beginning the weaving of the hammock, review Chapter 14 on loom weaving, in which the loom on which we wove this hammock is described and pictured in detail.

String or warp the loom with the sisal, using forty-one strands, wrapped entirely around the two sides of the loom. Space the strands about ¾ inch apart. This will make the hammock about thirty inches wide.

Beginning about five inches from the lower dowel, weave six rows of crimson jute across the warp strands, weaving over and under and reversing on the next row. Now you are ready to weave the cattails.

Here are some hints before you go on: Keep your outside warp lined up squarely or your hammock will pinch in the middle like an old-fashioned corset or hourglass. To prevent this narrowing, always lay the weft in *loosely.* Tying the outside warp strands to the side of the loom also helps to

Fig. 6-14. *This attractive hammock is made of sisal, cattails, and jute, the jute forming the bird pattern.*

keep it from tightening in. As you proceed, measure the width often to make sure that it remains the same all the way up.

Press or pound down the weft after every row of weaving with your fingers or a batten stick (see Fig. 14-2).

Remember that the very dry cattails will have to be soaked in water for five or ten minutes and then kept wrapped in a wet towel, leaves, or paper until used. Warm water works best and if you are out in the wilds, there are often sun-warmed ponds or creek shallows for this.

Freshly cut, green cattails can be used, and are great to work with, but more care should be taken in pounding them tight as you weave, for they will shrink about one-third after they dry and the weaving will be quite loose.

Now, with dampened cattails, weave about fifty rows, and then six more rows of the crimson jute.

These numbers we are giving are not to be considered a hard and fast rule that must be followed; they just happened to be the ones we used for this particular hammock. The beauty of weaving is that the article you are making can be your own creative design, and the descriptions of our weavings are to be used only as examples which you may or may not want to follow in detail. As a matter of fact, this hammock can be made entirely of cattails—a fast method of getting a hammock in a hurry. If we were out roughing it and needed to produce something to sleep on that would get us up off the ground and away from the ticks and snakes, a much cruder hammock would be our choice—all cattails or willow whips merely laid across the warp, or even bundles of grasses laid in the same way. Making the more complicated designs is slow going, and one who tackles them must have a great deal of patience.

But if you do have the time and patience to go in for design, the value of a handwoven item lies in the fact that no two are alike. Proof is the fact that when we first thought of making an Indian Thunder Bird design, I was amazed to discover that no two of the birds we found in pictures were alike. Ray, who has a regular library of early Americana books, hunted up a dozen or so pictures of the fabled Thunder Bird, all of them so stylized that they were only vaguely identifiable as such. Each artist had depicted his own version. Many were hardly identifiable as a bird of any sort; they were simply a sketchy hint of the idea. So we too allowed our imagination to hold sway and dreamed up a bird of our own. Practically anyone could have done better than this one, but no one could possibly have had more fun doing it.

We will give the pattern we followed, step by step, but believe you will find as you weave that your own creative ability will take hold and your own design will take on a flavor of its own.

As we point out in Chapter 14 on loom weaving, a shuttle is a handy thing to have for the weaving of such things as jute and other continuous long strands, but if you do not have one, there are other ways to solve the problem.

One simple method is to make a shuttle-sized bundle of weft by wrapping about six yards of it around your hand and lashing it into a narrow bundle, as in Figure 6-15, that will slip through the openings between the warp strands as though it were a shuttle. This works well when the warp is spaced as far apart as it is for this hammock. Ease out a couple of feet of weft as it is needed, from the shuttle bundle. If you prefer, a large needle may be used, but this takes longer to draw the lengthy strands through.

To begin the bird pattern, after the fifty or so rows of cattails have been woven in, count across from the side to the middle (the twenty-first strand).

Begin the crimson bird tail by weaving over and under the three middle warp strands, for three rows. Continue in lifts, or stairsteps, of three rows, shaping the bird tail out by including one warp strand on each side after every three rows. We made thirty rows of crimson for the tail.

For the lime green body, set in to the fourth warp strand from the

Fig. 6-15. *For widely spaced warp, the weaver can be bunched in this manner to serve as a shuttle, letting out weft as needed.*

90

outside edge of the crimson tail. Weave across to the fourth strand on the other side. This makes the lime row fifteen warps wide.

After weaving three rows of lime this way, drop one warp strand at each side and weave three more rows.

Drop a warp strand on each side and weave nine rows.

For the lower curve of the wing, weave across, adding a strand of warp on each side with each row, for twelve rows. This will leave four unwoven strands of warp on each side. Weave two more rows of this length for the wing tip and then start diminishing for the upper curve.

For three rows drop one strand, and then, to make the curve more abrupt, drop a warp strand and weave three equal length rows for five lifts with three rows in each lift.

For the brown edging, begin at the bottom and take in four warp strands in lifts of three rows, sewing in between each of the strands that has already been woven (a needle is necessary here); then for edging on the wing curves, take in only one warp strand.

Edge both sides of the bird, and then, for the head, again count from the side to the twenty-first warp strand and with brown weft, weave over and under two warps. Loop it over the third and weave back, taking in five warps. Continue weaving the five warps for nine rows; then take in two more warps at each side for three rows.

Go back to five warps for six rows; then again take in two more warps for three rows.

Now for the top of the brown head, take in three warps for six rows.

To finish the head of the bird, encircle it with the crimson jute, with a stylized impression of an opened bill at the right side.

Start the crimson at the right side of the head by weaving over two warp strands for six rows, sewing into the brown pattern.

To make the lower part of the bill take in two more warps for two rows, then three warps for one row, and then two warps for two rows.

Now go back to weaving over just two warps for another six rows. Make the upper part of the bill as you did the lower.

Continue on around the head, filling in around the brown pattern. The close-up photo in Figure 6-16 will serve as a good guide to refer to when in doubt.

Now thread up a large needle with four strands of raffia (or another color of jute or swamp grass) and proceed to fill in the warp around the bird. Again, watch those edges as you weave, for this is the most difficult problem of loom weaving: keeping those edges from pinching in.

Fig. 6-16. *To make this cattail hammock we warped a large loom with sisal (see Chapter 14 for directions on making the loom) and began weaving with cattails, using jute and raffia for the colorful pattern of the bird. However, we would not again use raffia, for it has a tendency to draw in moisture, and this part of the hammock is damp from dew in the morning.*

Finish off this section with about four rows of crimson jute or one of the other colors.

The stylized designs of Indian rug weaving are strangely intriguing, but not until you get into the weaving of such patterns yourself, do you realize the reason for this oddity: it is not by choice but by necessity that they are shaped as they are. The very nature of the weaving process calls for right-angle designing, for, unlike drawing, where the pen or brush can travel at any slant, the weaving lines must all take the horizontal. The design then, must proceed in lifts, and this in itself creates the unique designs not found in paintings.

Continuing with the hammock, swing the brace at the back forward, thus bringing the other side into position for weaving. Beginning at the bottom, repeat the entire design, with the exception that the bird's bill is on the left rather than the right. Don't forget the final four rows of crimson jute.

Now all that remains is to fill in the center section of the hammock with cattails.

Loosen the butterfly taps at the top of the loom, allowing the dowel to slip down the slots. The weaving is now loose enough to roll over the dowels, allowing the unwoven section of warp to move into a position for weaving.

The entire center is now filled in with cattails.

The hammock is ready to tie off. Cut the warp strands between the two ends of the hammock, a few at a time, and tie every two together over a dowel or stick, until all are tied. Repeat on the other end. Tying holds the weft in tight, and the dowel serves as a spreader for the hammock ends.

To make the end slings of the hammock, run sisal strands into the warp loops and gather them together in a bundle about two feet from the end of the hammock, as in Figure 6-17. Wrap them tightly with more sisal.

Fig. 6-17. The hammock ends are finished up by bundling and binding in this way.

These ends may be dyed, if you like, by the simple method of dipping them into hot dye. Sisal takes most dyes beautifully.

Another and neater (but more difficult) way to make the sling ends is by tying them in fishnet knots, as in Figure 6-18. Tie a pair of strands; then separating, tie the inner ones to the next, etc., decreasing as you go.

Fig. 6-18.   *Another type of hammock end is the fishnet tied.*

SHOULDER BAG

The shoulder bag in Figure 6-19 was made of cattail blades, woven in the diagonal braid pattern pictured in Figure 1-4. It is laced together with strands of dyed jute.

For the body of the bag, twenty-five cattail blades were placed in two groups on a flat surface, and woven diagonally over each other, as in Figure 6-20. In this case there are twelve blades on one side and thirteen on the other.

With the over-and-under weaving, weave the blades on a slant across the groups. When they are all woven together, bend forward the outside blade of the group of thirteen and weave it to the middle. (*Note*: This thirteenth blade must be in a position to bend forward *over* the one beside

Fig. 6-19. Shown here is a shoulder bag, woven of cattails in the diagonal pattern. This pattern is described in more detail in the section on making a braid hat in Chapter 4. Shell dogwood blossoms are trimming.

Fig. 6-20.   The shoulder bag is being woven in the diagonal pattern.

it. If it is not, then simply turn the whole thing over, back to front, so that it will be.)

After weaving this blade to the middle, there will now be thirteen on the other side. Again bend the thirteenth blade forward and weave it to the middle. Keep alternating sides, always weaving the outside blade from the group that has the largest number, until the weaving is thirty-six inches long.

It is unlikely that your cattail blades will be long enough to weave to that length; so, as each one is almost used up, insert a new blade and weave it in with the old one for several rows.

You now have a large braid mat about thirty-six inches long and twelve inches wide and pointed at each end—and looking not at all like a shoulder bag. But despair not; the worst is yet to come.

One of the points on the mat is to be left for the flap. Weave the ends of the blades back into the weaving. The other end is cut off and these blades too are woven back into the other weaving.

96

Now we are ready to make the handle and sides of the bag, which is actually merely a long strip of five-strand braid. As in the body of the basket, this braid is also woven on the diagonal as in Figure 1-4, but of five cattail blades, in groups of two and three.

Weave the braid to about sixty-six inches long, splicing where it is necessary. Bring the ends together and sew it in a loop.

Now, before adding the side braid, finish the top and flap of the bag by stitching it with a lashing of jute in the buttonhole stitch, as shown in Figure 6-21.

Place the joined section of the side-handle braid at the bottom of the bag and sew it through with thread or fine sisal. Then start lacing it with jute that has been threaded into a wooden needle, into the side of the bag.

A bag such as this can be left plain or trimmed with shells and (or) embroidery. On this one we have sewn sprays of white dogwood blossoms, made of rosecup sea shells. An olive shell, drilled and strung on jute, is the button for the clasp, which is a loop of jute. This loop is made by looping two strands of jute into the point of the flap, and making a buttonhole stitch over it.

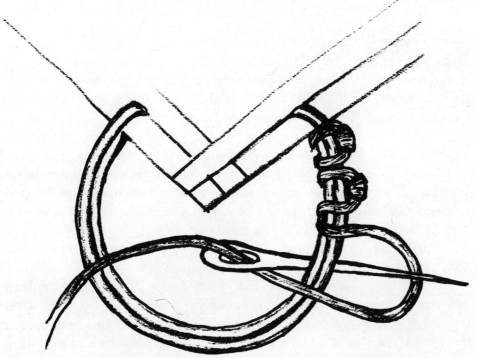

Fig. 6-21. *Jute was used in a buttonhole stitch to form the loop fastener for the shoulder bag.*

CHAPTER 7

Willow Whips and Vines

As with all wild materials, there are problems in weaving with willows and vines. The greatest fault with willows, is the fact that the limbs, or whips, taper from the end where they join onto the larger limbs, to the tip, thus causing problems with the uniformity of the weaving. However, in its favor, the willow whip is pliable and strong.

Weeping willows have the longest whips, but the new sprouts of creek willows that have been cut back are excellent weaving material as well.

Vines too have their problems, for they are often knobby where small branches occur along their length. However, here again there is one important point in their favor: they can be found in long lengths that taper very little, thus lessening the necessity to splice often.

Many kinds of vines are used for weaving—wild grape, honeysuckle, Virginia creeper, etc. Different areas offer various kinds.

It has been our experience that vines and willows that have been thoroughly dried are brittle and do not entirely regain their pliability when they are soaked in water. For this reason, we like to use these freshly cut, though it is possible to keep them pliable for several days by wrapping them in wet paper, leaves, or cloth.

For those craftsmen who live in tropical countries, there is rattan, bamboo, pandanus, and other excellent materials that can be used in the same way as willows and vines.

Willowwork, despite its name, is usually done with commercially manufactured pulp reed; this is, of course, easier to work with: more uniform in size, longer, and more pliable than the wild materials. But since we are primarily interested in the fun of collecting our own materials, we must substitute, attempting to awaken our dormant ingenuity and practice the inventiveness of our forefathers. The skills are there, unused for generations, but surprisingly eager to express themselves when called upon. Probably one of the easiest of the weaving styles is willowwork, and thus a good one for the novice to start with.

Willowwork is usually done with round spokes and weavers, with the spokes at least twice the circumference of that of the weavers; but a combination of round spokes and flat, soft weavers, or stiff, flat spokes and small, round weavers works as well. It is a matter of using whatever material you have available, so long as you remember that the spokes must be of a firmer material.

Have all material damp or freshly cut so that it will not break. However, in the event a spoke does break, it is easily spliced as in Figure 7-1.

BURDEN BASKET

In order to have their hands free, the Indians of America and other primitive peoples carried burdens in a carrier, or burden basket, held by a

Fig. 7-1. A broken spoke can be spliced by cutting on an angle and binding.

tumpline over the forehead. The basket was unique in shape, with one straight side, like that of a fish creel, but, unlike the fish creel, was designed to fit flat against the back.

The burden basket in Figure 7-2 was made by the wickerwork type weaving pictured in Figure 1-1. Willow whips were used for the spokes and the weavers. The binding on the rim and braid tumpline are of cattail blades. The variegated pattern is created by the simple method of using the entire length of the blade, from the creamy white base to the light green tip.

To make this basket, cut six willow whips, thirty-four inches long. Cross the six in two groups of three, and weave a cattail blade three times

Fig. 7-2. *Barney the cat seemed to think the burden basket was woven especially for him.*

around the groups of spokes, as in Figure 7-6. Now cut another spoke sixteen inches long and slip it down beside one of the others into the weaving, in order to have an uneven number. Now begins the over-and-under weaving as in Figure 7-8, forcing the spokes apart until they are in the form of a wagon wheel. Be sure that in each row the weaver crosses the spoke on the side opposite to the one it crossed before.

As you weave, begin to bend the basket spokes up for the sides. The burden basket has a flat side, and this can be formed by holding it against you.

During the weaving, the spokes become too far apart; this can be remedied by adding more spokes. Cut twelve more spokes, fourteen inches long, and push them down into the weaving beside the others, thus making twenty-five in all. Again force the spokes apart as you weave.

When there are only about three or four inches of spokes showing above the weaving, clip them all the same length and bend the ends over, laying them along the top of the basket. Lash a large cattail blade over them, with another cattail blade that has been threaded into a wooden needle.

The braid tumpline is made of diagonal braid as in Figure 1-4. Use

Fig. 7-3. This photo shows the partly woven cattail-willow burden basket and the tumpline, which will be added to hold it over the forehead. This basket is woven in the same manner as the wickerwork basket, described and pictured next, with the exception that the slope is more abrupt and one side is flattened to lie against the back.

101

five cattail blades for this, laying them on a flat surface in groups of two and three. Weave these over each other on a slant, and then, turn the outside blade of the section of three toward the front and weave it to the center. There will now be more blades on the other side. Turn the outside blade of this side to the front and weave it to the center. Continue until you have a strip of braid long enough to go around the basket twice, over the head, and down into the center. It will be necessary to splice the blades as they run out. Do this by weaving in a new blade with the old one for a couple of inches.

This braid is looped completely around the basket for added strength, and brought almost to the bottom on the inside. Sew it securely with a cattail blade or cordage, through both the inner and outer braids. This assures a strong carrier.

WICKERWORK BASKET OF FOUR MATERIALS

To demonstrate that practically any material may be used for this type weaving, we made a small bun basket of four different materials: willow whips, honeysuckle vine, cattails, and swamp grass. The bun basket on the right in Figure 7-4 is the result, and though it is not as perfect in structure

Fig. 7-4. *The partially finished basket on the right is woven of four different kinds of materials, proving that most anything that grows in the wilds can be used in some way in basket weaving. This is in the wickerwork or willowwork pattern. The basket on the left is made in the same way, but from pulp reed, which is more uniform to work with but cannot be found in the wilds.*

as the pulp reed one shown in the same illustration, there is satisfaction in knowing it was made of things we collected from the wilds.

For this basket, which is nine inches across and six inches high, begin by cutting six spokes, twenty-two inches long, of freshly gathered willow whips. Cross the six branches in threes, as in Figure 7-5.

Tuck the end of a weaver (a small honeysuckle vine, in this case) in under a spoke and hold it there as you wrap the weaver around the groups of spokes, as in Figure 7-6. This anchors the spokes for further weaving. Wrap over the groups of three spokes three times.

Now before beginning the over-and-under weaving as in Figure 7-8, it will be necessary to add another spoke, for an uneven number is required for this type of weaving. Cut this spoke only eleven inches long. Tuck it in under the weaving (see Fig. 7-7). Now you will have thirteen spokes.

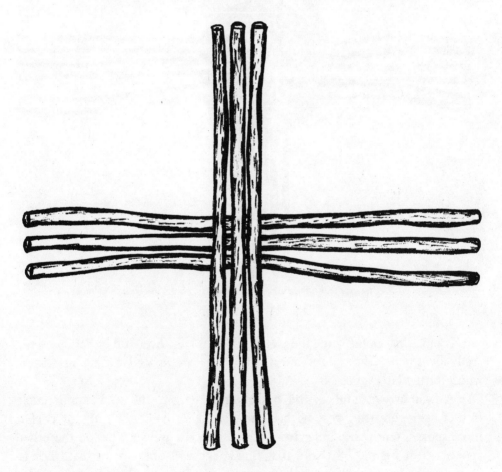

Fig. 7-5. For the willowwork basket, willow whip spokes are crossed in groups of three.

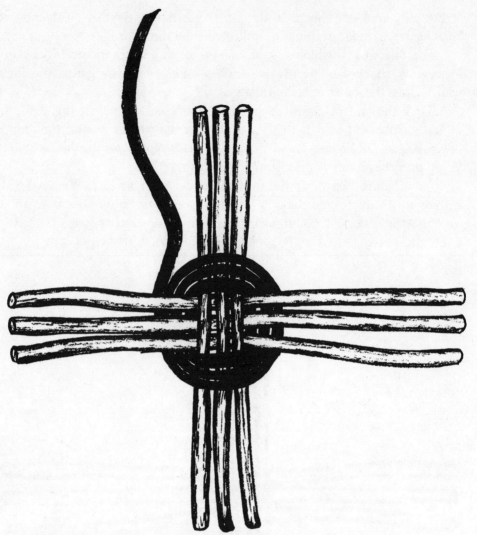

Fig. 7-6.   A weaver is looped three times around to hold the spokes in place.

From this point on, the weaver forms an over-and-under pattern, gradually forcing the spokes apart until they are spaced evenly in wagon wheel form, as in Figure 7-8.

As you weave, and as the basket grows larger, the spokes are much farther apart, and the weaving becomes too loose. At this point, cut twelve more spokes, ten inches long. Insert these into the weaving beside the other spokes, as in Figure 7-8. Note that one spoke will not have a mate beside it, for again it is necessary to have an uneven number. Now there will be

Fig. 7-7. *Another shorter spoke is added, for this type of weaving requires an uneven number of spokes. Arrow points to added spoke.*

twenty-five spokes. Continue weaving, forcing the spokes apart until they are evenly spaced.

When a weaver has almost run out, tuck another in beside it and continue weaving them together; then go on with the new weaver.

When you have a circle of weaving about six inches across, begin shaping the spokes up for the sides of the basket by bending them as you weave. If the spokes are dry, pause here to dunk them in a stream or bathtub for a half-hour or so while you revive yourself with a rest, for at this point they could break.

Continue weaving, shaping the spokes up in whatever slope you like. The basket sides may come up straight, slope out, or even curve in at the top; it's your prerogative.

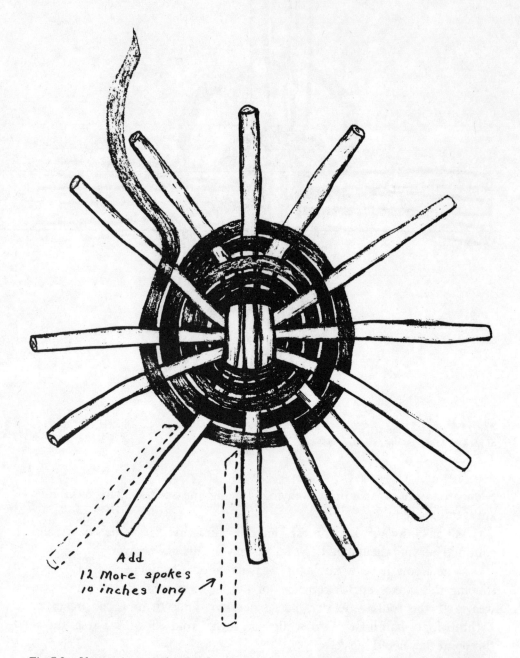

Add
12 More spokes
10 inches long

Fig. 7-8. Now start over-and-under alternate weaving and continue, adding more spokes between the others as the weaving becomes too widely spaced. It is still necessary to keep an uneven number of spokes; so add only twelve, and as you weave, work all the spokes out to a wagon wheel shape.

Continue weaving until there is about four inches remaining of the spokes. Again dunk the basket, especially the top, in water; and have another rest. It is important, at this point, that the spokes be quite pliable, for they will be getting quite a bending in a moment.

There are several ways to finish off the edge of a willowwork basket, but one of the easiest and most attractive is the following.

Bend a spoke in an arc and insert the end in the weaving beside the second spoke from it, as in Figure 7-9. Continue all around the basket. This makes a nice strong scalloped edge.

Another rim, that is more unique, is the one we have made for the basket on the left in Figure 7-11. We bent each spoke over until it lay along the top of the basket and bound it there by lashing a binding of cattail

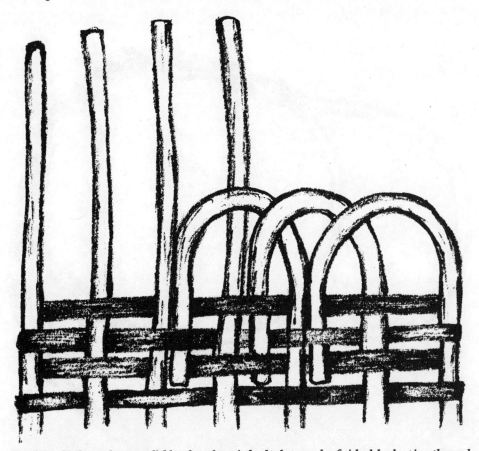

Fig. 7-9. *If the spokes are pliable, the edge of the basket can be finished by looping the ends and inserting them down into the pattern at every other spoke or every third one. This makes a nice scalloped rim. If the spokes are not limber, the rim will have to be bound as in the basket on the left in Figure 7-11.*

107

blades over the top, held with swamp grass. A darning needle is used for this, or a wooden needle.

For the base of this basket, form a loop three inches across in the middle of a willow whip. Then, holding the loop in your left hand, start wrapping the ends around the loop to make a twist, as in Figure 7-10. Keep wrapping until a three-strand hoop is completed. Now either glue the hoop to the bottom of the basket, or tie it in by looping sisal or other small cordage around the hoop and up into the weaving of the basket in several places.

This bun basket, made of four different kinds of materials, is now complete. But don't forget that there are many variations possible in both the materials and style of basket, and part of the fun in weaving is in dreaming them up for yourself.

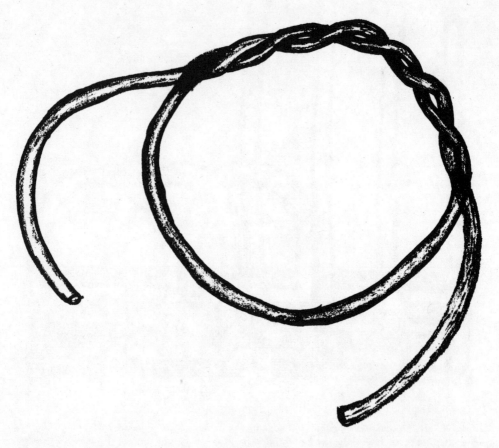

Fig. 7-10. *A base for the basket is made of a coiled willow whip. Keep coiling until it is a thick hoop and glue or tie it to the bottom of the basket.*

BASKET WITH RING-WEAVE TRIMMING

It is difficult to find material that works well for the attractive, lacy ring weaving used in the small basket pictured in Figure 7-11. It must be formed in small coils, and the material used must be both pliable and uniform in size. Unfortunately, materials in the wilds seldom have both these requirements. Manufactured pulp reed works nicely for this, but we wanted to use only native plants; so we did the best we could with willow whips, laced with swamp grass.

This was not an easy project for the willow whips were short, as they had to be cut from the middle of the branches to keep them from tapering too much. This, of course, required frequent splicing.

However, the finished basket turned out to be an interesting one, for ring weaving is seldom seen. Several rows of the sturdier coil weaving, like the lower part of the basket, finished off the top.

Fig. 7-11. The finished willowwork basket and a partly finished ring-woven basket.

HOT PADS

Willowwork weaving was the method used to make three of the hot pads in Figure 7-12, and willows were the spokes for two of them—the ones on the right and left. The hot pad in the center is also willowwork, or rather wickerwork, for it is not made of willows but is a mixture of ribs cut from Sabal palm fronds and narrow strips of the fronds. The upper pad will be described in Chapter 14 on loom weaving.

For the willowwork pads, we used spokes of small willow whips, and the weavers were of raffia, sisal, and jute.

As we have said before, using tree limbs—even the long, supple willow whips—presents a problem: they taper. The diameter of a willow whip will often decrease by half in the space of a couple of feet. For this reason,

Fig. 7-12. *These hot pads were made in various ways. The one at the top was made on a hoop stick loom (see Fig. 14-6), and the pads on the left and right were woven in the willowwork pattern, with willow spokes and jute and raffia weavers. The one in the center is made from ribs and strips of Sabal palm fronds.*

110

cut your spokes from the centers of the branches, trying to choose those sections that taper the least.

To begin, cut six spokes, fourteen inches long, and lay them in groups of three in a cross, as in Figure 7-5. Tuck the end of a strip of raffia in under the spokes, and wrap the raffia around the groups of spokes three times, tying them together as in Figure 7-6.

Since it is necessary, in this type of weaving, to have an uneven number of spokes, another must be added. Cut a shorter one about seven inches long and slip the end of it down between two of the other spokes.

You are now ready to weave over each of the spokes. Weave over and under alternately, forcing the spokes apart, until they are in the form of a wagon wheel.

Continue weaving over and under, making certain that the weaver crosses each spoke opposite from the way it did in the row before. For instance, if it went over a spoke in the row before, it should go under the same spoke in the following row.

To make the pad on the right of Figure 7-12, we continued to weave for a dozen or so rows with maise-colored raffia, and then changed, for color variety, to crimson jute for another couple of inches.

But before this point is reached, you will notice that the spokes are becoming too far apart for close weaving and more will have to be added. And this is the tricky spot. There is no problem in adding the spokes for they slip easily in beside the other ones, but the problem arises from the fact that, if one of these shorter spokes drops out after you continue weaving, it is difficult to see where it belongs and the pattern could go haywire. For this reason, push the new spokes far down into the weaving.

For the new spokes, cut twelve ten-inch spokes and insert them into the weaving alongside all but one of the original spokes. This is to keep the number uneven. You now have twenty-five.

Again, gradually force the spokes apart as you weave, to form the uniformly spaced wagon wheel, and continue weaving. We changed to a natural-colored sisal, and then a nut-brown jute.

When the mat is about nine inches across, and there are more than two inches remaining of the ends of the spokes, cut the weaver off and thread the end of it back into the weaving to anchor it.

Now for the edging. Curve each spoke over into an arc and slip the end down beside the one next to it, into the weaving. You may call it a day at this point, leaving the scallops of willows for an edge, or, as in the pad pictured, trim it with an edging of jute or sisal in a buttonhole stitch.

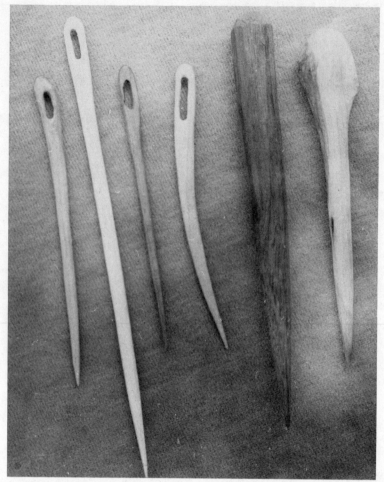

Fig. 7-13. Ray carved these needles and awls from hedge root. Wooden needles are far superior in basketry to steel, for they slip through the material with more ease without cutting it.

To make the buttonhole trim, thread a wooden needle or large darning needle with the cordage. In this pad we used crimson-colored jute.

Stitching down through two rows of the weaving, make a close buttonhole stitch, as in Figure 6-21, all around the pad. Then anchor the thread end by weaving it back an inch into the weaving and cutting it off.

FISH TRAP

The woven fish trap described below was made in one form or another by early man all over the world.

To begin the trap shown in Figure 7-14 we cut seventeen fifty-inch-long slender tree branches (an uneven number is needed) and bound the small ends together in a bundle. These spokes may be any green sprout or limb such as willow. For weavers we used vines. Most kinds of pliable vines will do, but we were fortunate in finding some of the most beautiful vines we have ever seen out on a wild Gulf of Mexico island. The vines, which are a member of the wood rose family, were of a uniform size and were running along the ground in the palm and pine forest to lengths of sixty feet. There were few if any branches on them—a real pleasure to work with.

Begin the weaving as in Figure 7-15, by putting two weavers together and weaving them by the over-and-under method for several rows in order to separate the spokes and align them in a wagon wheel form. After five rows of this, separate the two weavers and start the twined weaving, as depicted in Figure 1-12.

Fig. 7-14. *Pictured here is a fish trap of the type made by early Indians. This photo shows the throat or cone being inserted.*

113

Fig. 7-15. Begin the fish trap by tying together the spokes and then weaving with vines.

After the weaving has progressed to about fifteen inches, it will be necessary to insert a hoop in order to increase the diameter of the trap. Bind or wire it inside the trap. Sisal or even small, pliable vines will do for this.

After the spreader hoop has been installed, continue the weaving for another three rounds. At this point, and with the increase in the flare of the trap, the spokes will be too far apart for good weaving, and more spokes will have to be added.

Insert sixteen more spokes beside the others, pushing them down into the weaving as far as the hoop. This will now make thirty-three spokes.

Continue the twined weaving, separating the new spokes from the old as you work, until all are evenly spaced. Continue weaving for another twenty inches; then tie in another hoop about sixty inches in diameter. Weave to within three inches of the ends and add another hoop.

The cone or throat comes next. It is a miniature of the trap itself but with the small end open to allow entry of the fish. Twenty-four or more sprouts are used for the cone, and again the weavers are vines.

114

Bind the cone inside the trap, as in Figure 7-14. Wire works best but cord will do, if the spokes are scored or notched to keep the cord from slipping off.

Now form a small door at the side of the trap by cutting a five-inch section from one of the spokes, and clipping 2 of the twined weavers. Double the weavers back and secure them. To cover the door lace a vine or cord across it, and remove this when it is necessary to take out the fish.

The final step is to attach a strong cord or rope with which to lower and raise the trap in the water.

This trap is rather light in weight and should be weighted by tying rocks to the bottom, especially if it is placed where there is a current or tide. A plastic bleach bottle or a fishnet float can be used for a floating marker.

Fig. 7-16.   *With rope-carrying handle installed, Ray is ready to set the fish trap.*

CHAPTER 8

Reeds and Grasses

Down through the ages, the most-used material for basketry has been the grasses—not especially because they are the best but because they are so readily available. Varieties of grasses, far too many to name, grow in all parts of the world, from the tall, tough swamp grasses to the round-stemmed field grasses; and all can be used in basketry with various degrees of success.

The round-stemmed grasses are especially good to bundle into rods for a base for coil weaving, and the flat-bladed types work well as sewing strips and as weft for loom weaving of grass mats used as sleeping mats, floor covering, and shelter walls.

The swamp grass used for the weavers in the body of the small covered basket in Figure 8-2 has a flat, tough blade and is a favorite of ours; and the red-brown buckhorn, from which the trim of this basket was made, is another.

Other items in which we have used grasses are the sandals and scuffs in Figure 6-2, the jute-sisal-grass mat in Figure 11-4, and the wall panel in Figure 8-6.

Fig. 8-1. *One method of strengthening grass for weaving or cordage is to twist several strands together, double these, and allow them to twist. Continue until the cordage or rope is the desired thickness.*

SMALL COVERED BASKET

This little basket is made of willow whips for the rods and swamp grass for the weavers, with a dark, red-brown trim of natural-colored buckhorn weeds. The knob on the lid is a tiny coconut which is still nestled in its "wood rose" blossom. These undeveloped nuts fall from the trees during windstorms and make interesting trims for baskets and hats.

The weaving pattern for the main part of this basket is a simple coil stitch (see Fig. 1-8). The wooden needle is excellent for this. A large darning needle may be used as well, or even a smooth stick for an awl to

Fig. 8-2. *This little covered basket (eight inches across) is made of small willow whips in the coiled pattern and trimmed with a braid of glossy brown buckhorn weed. A baby coconut serves as a lid handle.*

117

enlarge the holes in order to insert the weaver, but this will be slower work.

The rim of the lid was whipped with the brown buckhorn weed, and a seven-strand braid trims the midsection.

To shape the basket up abruptly, simply stop adding stitches when the bottom has reached the desired size. For both the lid and the bottom, the number of stitches that will be needed to keep them flat will be a guessing matter. Lay the weaving down on a flat surface every few rows and, if it threatens to cup, add more stitches.

BRAID BELT

This interesting indigo and maize belt (see Fig. 8-3) is woven of dyed swamp grass in the diagonal braid pattern, pictured in Figure 1-4.

Fig. 8-3. *The grass belt, woven of indigo- and maize-dyed swamp grass in a diagonal style, makes an attractive plaid pattern. An olive shell with a jute buttonholed loop forms the fastener.*

The thirteen blades of this braid are woven in the same manner as that shown in Figure 1-4, but with seven blades on one side and six on the other. To make the plaid pattern, the first three grass blades on each side are maize-colored.

Weave the two groups of seven and six blades across each other on a slant (see Fig. 8-4), and then, turning the outside blade of the group of seven toward you, weave it across to the center. There will now be seven on the other side. Weave the outside blade of this group to the center and then continue, alternating sides in the same manner.

When the belt is three inches longer than the desired length, cut off the pointed ends and, turning them under, sew a hem.

The buckle is made of jute, but braided grass, sisal, or other cordage

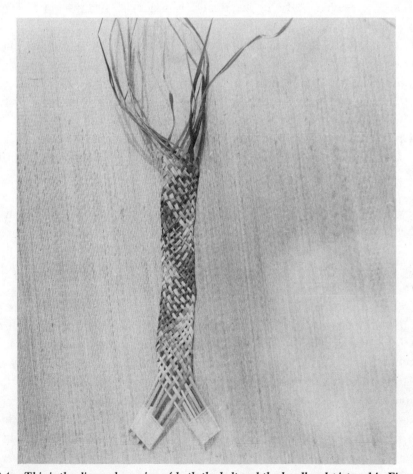

Fig. 8-4. *This is the diagonal weaving of both the belt and the headband pictured in Figure 8-5.*

could be used as well. For the buckle a half-loop is formed of two strands of cordage, sewn in at each edge of the belt. The loop is then strengthened by whipping it with cordage in a buttonhole stitch, illustrated in Figure 6-21.

The clasp is an olive shell but another type of shell could be used, or even a small piece of smooth wood. The shell has a hole drilled in the closed end and it is strung on cordage. Tie the cordage through the openings in the weaving of the end of the belt. The belt is fastened by looping the buttonhole-stitched hoop over the olive shell.

BRAID HEADBAND

Like the woven belt, the headband is made of swamp grass, dyed in maize and indigo blue.

Choose eleven long blades of the flat grass—five of one color and six of the other. Our grass blades, pictured in Figure 8-4, were long enough so that no splicing was necessary. But if your grass blades are not long enough, it is a simple matter to insert another blade of a like color and weave it with the last few inches of the old one.

Cross the two groups of five and six blades and weave them over and under together, as in Figure 8-4. To make the plaid pattern we put three indigo blades on the outside of each group. The colors crisscross as you weave, giving the headband the tweedy, plaid effect.

A suggestion: If we are weaving at home and not out in the woods somewhere, we use a clipboard to hold the ends of the blades as we weave; or they may be fastened with masking tape to a table or simply clipped together with a clothespin so that the weaving will not become disarranged.

When the groups of blades are woven together, check to be sure that the outside blades are in such a position that they are back of those next to them. The reason for this is that the outside blades are the weaving blades throughout, and all the weaving is done forward; so the outside blades must bend forward over the ones next to them. If these blades are not in back at this point, simply turn the entire thing over so that they will be.

Now bend the outside blade of the larger group forward and weave it across to the center, as in Figure 8-4. You will now have six blades on the other side. Bend the outside blade of that group forward and weave it across to the center.

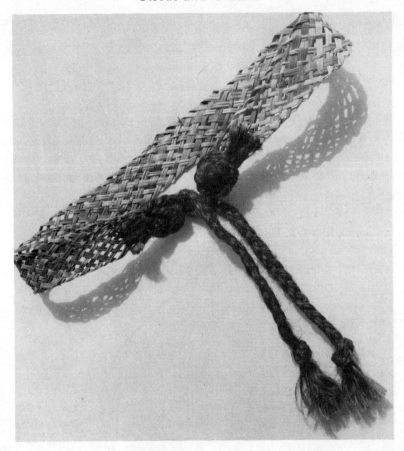

Fig. 8-5. The headband was finished off with jute ties.

Continue weaving the outside blades on alternate sides until the braid is twenty-three inches long—shorter if the headband is intended for a child.

Cut off the remaining ends, and grouping them closer, tie them together with thread. Do the same for the other end.

During the weaving, the grass blades have probably become dry, so at this point it is a good idea to dunk the last two inches on each end in water for a couple of minutes, for these are now bent back an inch and sewed under the headband.

There are several ways to make the fastener or tie for the band. A fastener can be made like that of the belt, with a buttonhole-stitched loop and a shell; or the braid can be woven long enough to lap over for tying. Another method, which we have used for this one, is to make two long, three-strand braids of dyed jute, tie them about an inch from the ends, and fray out the twist for tassels. Now curve the other ends of these braids into rosettes and sew them to the ends of the headband for ties.

GRASS WALL PANEL

Though the palm frond panel, described in Chapter 3, is probably the most quickly constructed, palm fronds are not available in temperate and northern zones; so a wall panel utilizing another material and weaving plan is described below.

For the following method we chose grass and sisal, but cattails, limbs from trees, vines, and other materials can be used as well.

There are many ways to weave these materials, but it seemed a good idea to fashion a loom that can be simply made from a tree and tree limbs, and once made, can be used over and over to quickly weave all the panels

Fig. 8-6. *One wall of our chickee was woven on a crude sling loom. It was made of sisal and tall grasses.*

122

needed to cover the wall of a shelter. This loom, though crude in operation, does away with the laborious system of weaving over and under each strand of warp, for it is so constructed that an opening wedge is created each time the working warp is raised or lowered, and the grass can simply be placed in this opening. We call this our "sling" loom.

To weave the grass panel in the following photos, choose a sturdy tree for the sling tying, nine strong stakes about four feet long to hold the stationary warp, and two end sticks about forty inches long.

To assemble the sling loom, notch one of the end sticks about three inches from the ends. This is to prevent the sling rope from slipping to the center. Tie on the sling rope and then tie it to the tree or another stationary object, as in Figure 8-7.

Fig. 8-7.   *Ray has tied the warp to the sling loom.*

Drive the nine stakes deep into the ground about three inches apart, lined up about eighty inches from the sling stick.

Now tie nine strands of sisal to the sling stick and to the stakes, as in Figure 8-7.

The eight strands of "working warp," which are now tied at the sides and between the stationary warp, must be at least eighteen inches longer than the stationary warp (or ninety-eight inches), for some of their length is used up during the weaving. With these strands tied, the loom is ready for operation.

Because of its length, it takes two people to operate this loom efficiently (see Fig. 8-8), though a small one of the same type takes only one person (see Fig. 14-7).

The working warp is lifted and a sheaf of six or eight blades of grass placed on the stationary warp in the open wedge created by the lift. This grass is then pushed up tight between the warp strands with the fingers or a batten board or even a couple of sticks.

Fig. 8-8. It takes two to operate a sling loom of this length. One raises and lowers the working warp and the other lays the sheafs of grass across the stationary warp.

Fig. 8-9.   After the wall panel is woven, the ragged edges of grass are trimmed.

Now lower the working warp to the ground and again place a sheaf of grass in the opening thus created, push it in tight, and lift the strands for another insertion of grass.

Repeat this process during the entire weaving, packing in each sheaf of grass as tight as possible as you work.

When the stationary warp is filled to the end, remove its strands from the stakes and tie them and the working warp to the end stick to complete your panel.

This panel may also be used as a hammock or as a floor mat. For the hammock or wall panel, the end sticks are left in; but if it is to serve as a floor mat, the end sticks are removed and the ends of the mat finished off by tying every two warp strands together.

One further word: to make the panel more durable, it is wise to weave in strands of sisal across with the grass at intervals and tie them to the outside warp on each side. This will prevent the warp from spreading to the

125

sides with use. This is especially important if the panel is to be used as a hammock.

There are two ways to weave in these cross strands of sisal. One way is to include a strand with about every sixth sheaf of grass and tie it at the sides. The other is to weave the entire panel and then, with a large needle, weave the strands across and tie them. We think the first method is the most practical.

The finished panel, woven on the above loom, is about thirty-two inches wide and seventy-five inches long, but of course can be made shorter on this same loom by simply not weaving to the end.

CHAPTER 9

Pine Needles

Some of the finest woven items are made of pine needles. These are comparable to the beautiful works of the weaving art produced by the Indians of America from the quills of the porcupine, an animal once in abundance and now rarely seen.

We described the type of pine needles that work well for weaving in Chapter 2, but will repeat: the longer the needles the better.

Pine needles are usually used as a rod base for coil-type weaving, especially in the furcate pattern as pictured in Figure 1-11. Most of the pine needle items pictured in the following pages were made in this manner, with raffia used for the sewing.

PINE NEEDLE BAG

For the weaving of the attractive bag shown in Figures 9-2 and 9-5, you may use the same stitches and designs as those described in the directions for making the bun basket, which follow, or use your imagination.

Fig. 9-1. *Here is a display of lovely pine needle work.*

One exception: after the first few rows of the furcate stitch around the large circles on the sides, start using the wheat stitch. This is done like the furcate with an additional stitch at each side, for the spacing of a large circle becomes wider as the circle widens and more fill-in is needed.

Good handles can be made of four rows of furcate-stitched pine needles with the edges trimmed with buttonhole stitch.

128

Fig. 9-2. This attractive bag was made of pine needles and raffia.

The bag pictured here was made up of two large circles of wire 11 inches across; a long oval strip, 4 inches wide and 27 inches long, that curves around the circles for the rim; 4 halved wooden balls, about ¾ inch wide, glued to the bottom for feet, and the handles. If a top is desired, it can be a shorter version (4 inches by 8 inches) of the oval strip.

Join the rim to the large circles by whipping with raffia. When the bag is completed, spray it with lacquer. This will stiffen, protect the finish, and add life to the bag.

Now you are ready for the lining, which is made in the same pattern as the large circles and long oval, allowing for seams.

The attractive napkin holder in Figure 9-3 is woven over a wire frame that may be made and soldered together or purchased in some craft shops. The designs of the basket are also good here.

Fig. 9-3.   This napkin holder is an ingenious example of pine needle work.

Fig. 9-4. *The bun basket and two pin cushion holders pictured here are made of pine needles and raffia.*

Fig. 9-5. *This is a view of the rim of the pine needle bag shown in Figure 9-2.*

Fig. 9-6.   *The side of the pine needle bag is shown here in close-up detail.*

PINE NEEDLE BUN BASKET

Of all basketry, we consider pine needle weaving the most intricate and delicate. It is actually a sewing art comparable to the work done with Battenberg and point lace stitching.

The bun basket in Figure 9-7 is a case in point, as you will see by

132

studying the center star and ring design. The materials used here are long pine needles sewn with raffia. We have effectively used sisal that we pounded out of agave blades for such sewing, though the several threads of the sisal are not as easy to work with as the raffia. Embroidery thread or twine will also work. For a cruder, rougher type of weaving, grass or strips of any plant that is strong and fibrous, such as milkweed stems, will do. And the patterns can be quite simple.

To begin this bun basket, thread a long narrow strand of raffia into a darning needle or a small wooden needle and cover six small (¾-inch) and two slightly larger (1-inch) brass rings with the double buttonhole stitch, pictured in Figure 9-9.

Now work spiderwebs (Figure 9-10) in the centers. These may be figures of your own designing.

The star is made by wrapping a piece of wire around nails driven into a board and soldering the ends of the wire.

Fig. 9-7. *In this pine needle bun basket the star and circles are formed over wire. Brass curtain rings are sometimes used.*

Fig. 9-8. *The furcate or chain stitch is illustrated above. A gage, made of a small section of plastic sipper or aquarium hose (such as that used with aerators), is just right to shape the sheaf of pine needles and hold them together as you work. Slip new pine needles into the gage as the others are used up.*

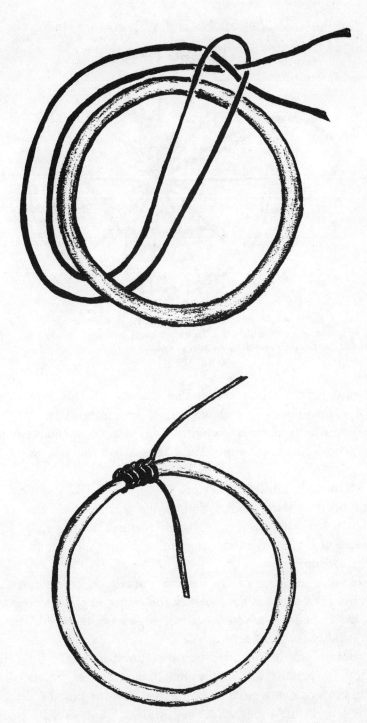

Fig. 9-9. Shown above are the steps in covering a ring or star with the double buttonhole stitch. Top: Fold a long strip of raffia in half and form a loop. Bottom: Cast a loop on the ring with the top strand of raffia and then cast another on with the lower strand. Keep alternating until the ring is covered. No needle is needed for this.

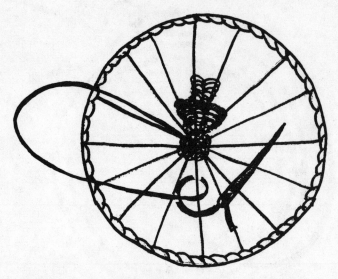

Fig. 9-10. Thread a thin strand of raffia into a needle, sew in as many spokes across the hoop as you wish, and then weave in spiderwebs. There are many patterns one can use. This one has four sections, but the fun is in creating your own designs.

It is next covered with the double buttonhole stitch, then fastened inside a large ring, about four inches across. The sections are now ready to join together with spiderweb patterns. You may copy the ones pictured here or use your own imagination. We like this pattern. It's simple and yet attractive.

With the center finished, the work goes quickly. Using a sheaf of eight or ten pine needles, start winding and sewing them around the center section of the basket with the furcate stitch pictured in Figure 1-11, at first keeping the bottom flat, then shaping and tightening up for the sides, and lastly flaring the rim.

The handles are formed by looping out the last two rows of pine needles at the ends of the oblong basket and filling in the opening with the medium-sized rings (which you previously covered with the double buttonhole stitch) and spiderweb stitches.

Other lovely pine needle articles are pictured in Figure 9-1. These are made basically the same way as the bun basket, and as we stated, can be designed as simply or intricately as you desire. If your pine needle basket is to be made out in the woods, with only wild materials available, and without the addition of wire and rings and raffia (which is only wild in certain areas of the world), the pine needles may be sewn with fine strips of fibrous plants (such as milkweed), using a needle whittled from a sliver of wood.

Fig. 9-11. *You may use this close-up detail of star and rings of the bun basket shown in Fig. 9-7 as a point of departure for your own imagination.*

CHAPTER 10

White Oak Splints

The following pages give the methods of master craftsmen in the weaving of split white oak. As we have stated before, there are other trees which may be used for this purpose; but our craftsmen (whose shops are on Missouri's Lake of the Ozarks) have proved to us by the beautiful baskets they weave, that they know what they're talking about, and we'll accept their word that white oak is the best tree for this purpose.

Methods for weaving can be found in Chapter 2. The photos in this chapter depict in detail the Ozark craftsmen's methods of splitting and weaving these splints.

MARKET BASKET

The check-woven rectangular basket in Figure 10-4 is one of the more simple splint baskets to make, for the check weave pattern requires spokes and weavers of the same size splints.

Fig. 10-1. *Most of these are baskets made of split white oak at a basket shop near Missouri's Lake of the Ozarks.*

Fig. 10-2. *There are only a few remaining craftsmen who still practice the art of split weaving in the United States. Here one of them rips boards from a white oak log with an ancient froe.*

Fig. 10-3. With drawknife, our craftsman begins to split out splints from a white oak board.

Fig. 10-4. A finished market basket is bound at the rim.

Rip out splints about 1½ inches wide. If the splints you have are narrower or wider, simply add or subtract the difference in width in determining the number needed to make a basket about twelve by twenty inches in size. Don't forget that width is added with the weaving. For instance, a side made with eleven 1½-inch splints will be about eighteen or twenty inches long (depending on how tightly you weave).

For the basket pictured in Figure 10-4 sixteen splints 1½ inches wide were used. Eleven of these were thirty-two inches long and five were forty-four inches long.

To begin, weave the five splints across the eleven. There will now be thirty-two spokes. Make certain that the woven section is in the center, with the spokes the same length all around. Now turn all the spokes up, forming the rectangular basket, and begin weaving another strip of splint around the side. Tuck in, glue, or staple the ends where they lap. To make a really

142

Fig. 10-5. Here a form has been constructed to facilitate the shaping of a split market basket, though such baskets are often woven without.

neat basket, start the weaving at the middle of the side where the splicing will be hidden by the handle.

Continue weaving until there are about two inches of the spokes left.

The top may be finished in one of several ways. If your spokes are quite pliable and will not break when making a sharp bend, you may simply bend them over and weave them down inside the basket. For the type of rim pictured in the basket in Figure 10-4, the spokes are all clipped evenly

Fig. 10-6.   *Depicted above are more styles of split-woven baskets.*

144

Fig. 10-7.   *These split-woven baskets have unusual shapes.*

Fig. 10-8.   *Another useful item made from split wood is this round wastebasket.*

at the edge of the rim and stapled or glued to the top weaver; then, for added strength and trim, the rim is bound with a narrow splint.

The handle is a long strip of splint which goes entirely around the basket. It can be worked into the weaving at completion, or woven in from the beginning.

Other shapes and styles of splint wood baskets are pictured in Figures 10-6, 10-7, and 10-8.

Fig. 10-9.   *Here our craftsman uses split white oak to weave a chair bottom.*

CHAPTER 11

Sisal

There are several materials, available from nature, that make good cordage —jute, from the jute plant; grasses of various kinds; raffia, that is obtained from the *Raphia pedunculata* palm, and others—but many are only to be found in certain areas of the world, and if these are to be used in weaving, they will have to be purchased by most people from hobby shops.

However, the agave plant, from which sisal (an excellent fiber) is made, occurs in many areas, and quite prolifically in tropical and semi-tropical zones.

In Chapter 2, we have described the crude but effective process we use to extract the fiber from the plant, and the twisting method used to make cordage. It isn't easy, but then few things worth doing are easy. And it is an amazing sight to see revealed those lovely white fibers from the big green blade of a plant.

We first learned this method from some boys in Old Mexico, and, delighted to find the plant growing in the southern United States, began making sisal ourselves, trying to emulate their quick, efficient movements.

Sisal is used in endless ways in Mexico, serving as the material for

Fig. 11-1. *Watch the stickers on the agave leaf when you cut it for making sisal. However, they are easily sliced off as they are only on the extreme edge.*

most of those colorful hammocks, woven mats, and other items you find in shops. We too use sisal in many ways, but the most important of these is in loom weaving. The hammock in Figure 6-16 and the small mat in Figure 11-4 both have warp of sisal.

LOOM-WOVEN MAT

For the mat in Figure 11-4, sisal, swamp grass, and jute were used. The sisal and jute can be pounded from the fibers of the agave (maguey) plant and jute plant, if you are in the localities where these grow, and twisted into cordage, as described in Chapter 2; or they can be purchased at hobby shops by the roll.

The loom can be a small rectangle of four boards or sticks, or one of the more complicated manufactured types. We have used the crudest stick

148

loom and the finest of the store-bought ones, and our weaving was as good on one as on the other. The loom used to make the mat in Figure 11-4 was a converted artist's easel.

The warp strands, which in this case were the sisal, can be looped over rods tied at either end of the loom; or each strand tied on the end boards of

Fig. 11-2. *Pounding out the sisal from the pulp is not easy but it's fun, and it seems almost a miracle to see the white fibers emerge from the pulpy green leaf. The blade is laid on a log and a stick used for the pounding.*

Fig. 11-3. *To make cordage from the sisal, twist several strands together and then, grasping them in the middle, allow them to twist together. This can be repeated to make thick rope.*

the loom, or, as we have done here, can be looped entirely around the loom—a fast but rather wasteful method, for some of the sisal at the back will have to be cut away. However, do allow at least four inches more sisal warp on each end than the desired length, for the extra will be needed to tie off as fringe.

For this mat (twelve by sixteen inches) twenty strands of sisal are looped around the loom, ¾ inch apart.

Thread a long strand of jute in the weaving sword or needle. For the latter use a section of cattail stem with a hole in one end, or a carved wooden needle.

Now begin the over-and-under weaving, bringing the jute across the sisal alternately under and over each strand.

Weave twelve rows, checking after each row to make certain it is woven alternately to the one before.

Each row of weaving must be pushed down tight against the one before. If you were using a conventional loom, with all the accouterments that come with it, you would have a batten stick (a bladelike board as pictured in Figure 14-2). For this small mat, the fingers, cupped into the warp, or a table fork will serve.

Now weave fourteen rows of swamp grass, using two blades of the grass in each row, if it is narrow. Then comes fifty rows of jute.

Now for the diamond design in the center, that gives the weaving the appearance of a Navaho Indian blanket or rug. Count to the two middle strands of sisal warp and weave the jute over and under them in a figure eight. Do this three times; then loop the jute weft over the next warp strand, weave across, and take in the fourth strand on the other side.

You are now weaving over four strands of warp. Again weave three

Fig. 11-4.   *This small mat was made of sisal, jute, and swamp grass.*

rows, take in the next warp strands at each side, and weave over the six for three rows.

Continue on up until you have woven over all the warp except two strands at each side, as in Figure 11-6.

The same process is repeated to form the top half of the diamond, with

Fig. 11-5. *The makeshift loom on which the mat is woven is in reality an artist's easel. A picture frame or even four sticks fastened together will work as well.*

152

Fig. 11-6. *A detail close-up of the weaving of the diamond figure in the small mat.*

the exception that you are now decreasing at the same rate as you increased stitches.

When the jute diamond is completed, thread the weaving sword with swamp grass and fill in at the sides of the diamond pattern, as in Figure 11-6.

The upper part of the mat is simply a repetition of the lower.

Now, with the weaving completed, remove the mat from the loom and tie off every two strands of warp. This secures the weft and also serves as a fringe trim.

Trim the fringe evenly with scissors, and your mat is completed.

Other designs and other materials can be used with this same weaving technique. The other mat pictured in Figure 6-1 was woven on this same loom, but of natural and yellow-dyed sisal, green cattails, and field grass of a natural yellow color. Though not as uniform in its weaving as the jute-sisal-swamp grass mat, it is attractive in its own way.

153

CHAPTER 12

Tree Bark

When you weave from bark stripped from trees, the size and strength of the basket will, of course, depend on the width and length of the bark strips. Long strips will work up to best advantage, but if shorter ones must be used (or if one breaks during the weaving process), they can be spliced quite efficiently. Simply hide the place where the strips join under a cross strip.

The methods of stripping and preparing bark strips can be found in Chapter 2. In the following pages we have given the step-by-step directions and illustrations for the weaving of a small, square basket in the check-weaving pattern—one of the best patterns for bark weaving.

BASKET WITH COLOR CONTRAST

For the small, sturdy bark basket in Figure 12-1, we used two kinds of bark in order to have a color contrast. The lower part is made of creek willow bark and the dark upper section is of slippery elm. All the original spokes are of willow bark. The rim is formed over a weeping willow limb.

Fig. 12-1. *Finishing off the bark basket is merely a matter of bending over the spokes and weaving them back inside.*

For a basket this size, start with sixteen strips of bark, about twenty inches long and about half an inch wide.

Weave these together in the check-weaving method, as in Figure 12-3. The woven part now forms the bottom of the basket. Bend the spokes up as you start weaving around the sides of the basket. At this point, you may either join each weaver, where it laps, and use another for each row, or you may add another spoke, to make an uneven number, and continue weaving the long strips as long as they last, splicing only when you run out. If you do not have an uneven number, the rows will not alternate in the over-and-under pattern but will all go in the same place. For this reason, insert another strip of bark about seven inches long between two of the other spokes.

Continue weaving over and under on alternate rows. When a weaver runs out, work another in with the end of it and continue.

Weave on up the sides until there is only about 2½ or 3 inches of spokes left. Now, cutting a willow whip that is about ¼ to ½ inch in diam-

Fig. 12-2. *Ray strips bark from a newly cut elm sprout.*

eter, make a square of it. To get it the right size, measure along the side of the basket and bend it at the corners. Taper the ends, where they meet, with a knife, and bind them together with fine cordage or thread.

Clip all the spoke ends to points and, bending each over the willow square, weave it back into the basket, with the ends on the inside, as in Figure 12-1.

Fig. 12-3. *Begin the basket by crossing the spokes and weaving them together. Then continue by bending up the spokes to form the sides.*

157

A handle may be added by looping a strip of bark, cattail, or palm frond into the rim between the openings of the weaving, and binding the ends closed. To make an even stronger handle, one of the original spokes in the middle of the basket sides can serve. Have this spoke extending out much longer than the others (about eight inches on each side). Then instead of weaving it over the willow square, loop it over in a hoop and bind the ends with a strip of bark, cattail, or frond.

CHAPTER 13

Leather

Though leather is not generally thought of as a material to be used in weaving, the early American Indian wove a wide variety of useful and decorative articles from it. The reason is apparent when you consider the fact that though animal life was widespread in those days, hides were not easy to take, nor was tanning those hides a snap. There was quite a process to go through, with the chewing of the hides, to soften them, one of the many steps. Obviously then, every scrap of that leather that had been attained only through a long, hard hunt and longer curing labor was used in some way, and some clever person discovered that one excellent way to utilize even the many small scraps was to weave them together.

Because we have seen many of the ancient woven items, it seemed that leather weaving must at least be touched upon in a book on weaving. And too, with deer hunting constantly gaining in popularity, in this modern day, there is always the question of what to do with those beautiful hides.

The hides can, of course, be tanned by a professional and made into jackets, moccasins, and gloves; or you can even, in an adventurous spirit, try tanning one of them yourself. Recipes for this can be found at your

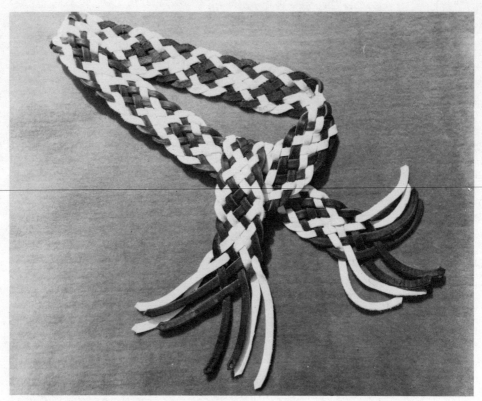

Fig. 13-1.   A belt woven of white and brown leather in the diagonal pattern.

local library. It just might be good for our morale to get an idea of the things early man went through simply in order to sustain life; it might make us appreciate our own easy living.

But whether you have the hides tanned or try it yourself, *all* of the hide can be used in some way. The small pieces can be cut into thongs or strips, even the squares, by the simple method of circular cutting, as shown in Figure 13-2.

These strips can be used in endless ways, but here we are considering them primarily for weaving. In loom-woven items, strips of leather can serve as the warp or weft or both. For diagonal finger weaving (see Fig. 13-1 for an example), there is no better material than these strips of leather.

Bags, belts, moccasins, headbands and hatbands, and even much larger articles are possible with this weaving. The size is determined simply by the size of the strips and the number used.

160

BELT

For the woman's belt in Figure 13-1, we used 8 strips of leather 65 inches long and ¼ inch wide (these may be spliced if necessary) in the diagonal, finger-weaving pattern.

The use of two contrasting shades of leather makes this pattern. A different design could be formed by using more colors, or placing the strips differently. The number of colors and their distribution determine the design on all finger weaving.

In this belt there are four white strips and four strips of very dark brown. The brown are placed all together in the center, with two white strips at each side. As the weaving proceeds, the colors cross over each other, forming the design.

Start the belt by placing the left group of four strips on a slant over those on the right. These may be held, for easier weaving, by gripping the

Fig. 13-2. *Small squares of leather can be cut in circles to make long continuous strips for weaving.*

ends on a clipboard, taping them down to a table, or pinning them to a cushion. Weave these over and under until they are all woven together, as in Figure 13-3. Now the diagonal weaving begins.

Begin by bending the left outside strip forward and weaving it over and under to the center. Now do the same with the right outside strip and again with the left. Continue weaving, alternating sides until all the strips

Fig. 13-3. *The long strands of leather are bundled to make weaving easier. If this is not done, they will tangle badly.*

162

are woven in to within about 2½ inches of the end. These ends will serve as fringe.

Trim the ends evenly and clip them in points. To fasten the fringe so that it will not unravel, either put a drop of glue under each of the crossing strips, or tack them with a needle and thread.

With a buckle added, this belt would be equally attractive for a man. In this case the ends are clipped square and bound with thin leather, with the buckle fastened in on one end with the binding.

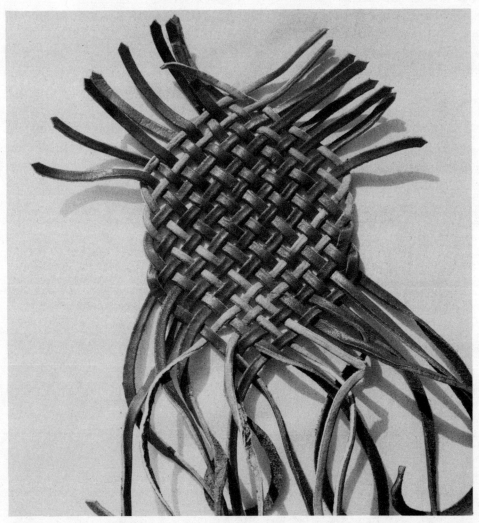

Fig. 13-4. *A woven leather pocket is an interesting trim for a jacket or skirt. The lower point can be left with the fringe, and the top cut off square and bound with a wider strip of leather.*

POCKET

A swanky trim for a jacket, wool skirt, or slacks is a woven leather pocket or a pair of them. These may of course be made any size, by adding to the number of strips or varying the cut size.

The pocket in Figure 13-4 is woven in the same manner as the above belt, but with 18 strips of leather, ¼ inch wide and 12 inches long.

Shades of brown and tan leather form the plaid pattern, but these too may be varied, with more contrasty colors making a more definite design, or all one shade showing only the weaving design itself.

For the top of this pocket, you may either clip the fringe short and use it as for the ends of the belt, or clip it off entirely and bind it around the point with a soft strip of leather. Or, if you want the pocket to be squared off at the top, simply cut the point off and bind the edge. For binding you may also use a strip of the material from which the garment is made that the pocket is to be used on.

The fringe on the bottom can be secured from raveling by gluing the strips where they cross over each other, or tacking them with a needle and thread.

CHAPTER 14

Loom Weaving

Weaving on a loom is one of the most fascinating of all the methods of weaving; the pattern possibilities are endless. One can be wildly imaginative, as with a wall hanging made up of many kinds and colors of grasses with odd things woven in, such as shells, seedpods, and even sticks and rocks—very mod. Or a loom-woven article can be a beautiful rug or mat resembling those woven by the Navaho Indians of the western United States, with the pattern formed by the placement of the weft strands, as in Figure 6-16.

This chapter constitutes a brief résumé of the art of weaving with looms, as it has been done in the past and present, discussing several types of simple looms, and following with some articles woven on them.

There is no doubt that ancient man was using weaving looms many thousands of years ago—probably, in the beginning, a crude affair of four sticks tied together at the ends into a square. But this statement is not intended as derogatory; our ancestors were pretty smart people, and the four-stick weaving loom is still a good one. This general idea, even in this automated day, is in use in various forms and is still the basic design for looms. Even with all the fancy innovations, the principles of loom weaving remain the same.

There are two groups of threads used: one group held taut (the warp), and the other, applied across it at right angles (the weft), forming a mesh which can be woven close or loose, as the weaver desires.

Even though the principles of loom weaving have not changed, looms do come in dozens of forms. They can be mere boards, with nails driven in, in the form of a square, rectangle, or circle; made of slotted cardboard; sticks hung on a tree limb; an arched limb with the ends sunk into the ground, and many more.

We have chosen to present only the most simple, since we are dealing, in this book, primarily with the weaving of materials that are obtainable in the wilds. We want it to be possible for the reader to go out into the woods, and with only his little hatchet, construct all the woven articles that would be necessary to survival. But we would also like to slip in a few hints on the weaving of articles one would be proud to keep and use for years.

Of the wild materials, several are adaptable for cordage for the warp of looms. Of course almost anything from thread to rope can be used for this; it will depend upon the use. If the article is to have heavy use, the warp must not be too fragile, though, since there is strength in numbers, small cords multiplied by the many required in loom weaving will bear a surprisingly heavy load.

Sisal, pounded from the agave plant and twisted into cord, as in Figure 11-3, makes a tough, durable material—but scratchy. Jute (though not available in as many areas as sisal) also makes a great cord, and is soft and pleasing to the touch. Both jute and sisal cord can be purchased in hobby shops if they do not grow in your locality.

But let's not overlook the lowly grasses, which are available to everyone, everywhere. At first thought, a blade of grass would seem far too crisp and fragile, but appearances are deceiving. Though one blade of grass is certainly too weak to hold anything, several twisted together (again as in Figure 11-3) produce a tough cord or rope which, though rather stiff, will nevertheless tie into a knot and can be used for both warp and weft in loom weaving.

Braided grasses and rushes and palm fronds can also be used for warp, with the single blades as weft, though the braiding is much more time-consuming than twisting the grasses.

Indians often used leather thongs for warp, with grass or other plant material for weft, in the weaving of sleeping mats, shelter walls, and floor mats. And for blankets and clothing they used the loom in one form or another to weave plant fiber of thread size.

EQUIPMENT FOR LOOMS

As we mentioned above, the loom itself can take many forms, though it is generally simply a square, rectangle, or round frame, but it is good to know that there are additional items of equipment that make weaving easier and less time-consuming. Several of these are described below.

The Heddle

The heddle is one such item, and it too comes in several forms. The rigid heddle (see Fig. 14-1) is made up of a row of thin slats, fastened to a frame. The holes are for one set of warp and the slots between the slats are for the other. Thus, when the heddle is lifted, it brings one set of warp up, opening a space (or shed) for the easy inserting of the weft. When the heddle is lowered, it opens up a shed with the other set of warp raised. This makes it possible to weave without laboriously working the weft over and under each strand of warp.

A much simpler heddle, though not quite as effective, can be made of

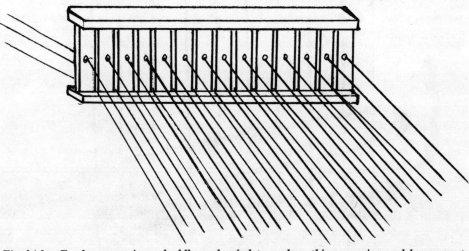

Fig. 14-1. *For loom weaving, a heddle made of slats, such as this one, raises and lowers warp for weaving, saving much of the labor of the over-and-under method. We did our weaving the hard way.*

one or two dowel sticks, or smooth tree branches. The sticks are tied to the two sets of warp (every other warp strand to a stick) with short strips of cord (about 10-inch) and operated by lifting the stick with one hand as you insert the weft with the other. If two of these heddle sticks are used, the second one will be lifted on the next row, opening another shed. However, some weavers prefer to use only one heddle stick, and then weave over and under on the row not controlled by the heddle.

Batten Stick and Comb

To make the weaving tight, something is needed to press weft close after the weaving of each row; here too, this item can be complicated or simple. For the large, intricately constructed looms, the batten board is built in, but it can be merely a hand-held slat or stick.

The batten board in Figure 14-2 is made from a thin board, shaped even thinner on the edges, and smoothed. Actually this board can serve a

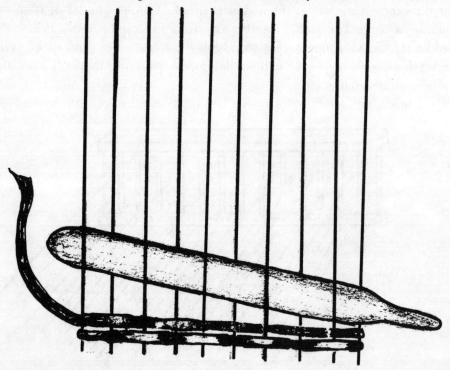

Fig. 14-2. *A batten board packs the weft down after each addition. In some cases a stick that has been smoothed, a fork, or even the fingers will do. We did not have a batten board for any of the work pictured in this book.*

dual purpose for, when turned edgewise, it will pound down the weft, and, when turned on its side, it will open up a shed between the sets of warp.

A wide-toothed comb or a table fork also works well to batten down the weft. You can even use your fingers, though we must admit it is rather hard on the fingers.

HOW TO MAKE A LOOM

If you are constructing a temporary loom in the wilds, tree limbs can be had for the cutting; but if you are doing your weaving at home, a more permanent one can be made of boards.

Board Loom

The lightweight but sturdy loom pictured in Figure 6-16 was designed and made by Ray in one evening. The beauty of this loom is that, even though it is quite large (forty by thirty-six inches), it can easily be taken apart for storage. Also, because of a clever placing of dowels, slots, and thumb screws, his design permits the making of an article, woven in a continuous strip, twice as long as the loom.

The sides of this loom are made of two 40-inch boards, which are 2 inches wide and ¾ inch thick. The braces at the back are of the same size boards, but only 36 inches long. The top and bottom of the loom are 1-inch dowels, 36 inches long. Round dowels were used for this, in place of boards, for it is on these that the warp is wrapped. A half-finished strip of weaving can easily be pulled forward over a round dowel in order to continue the weaving.

To make the slipping of the weaving easier, the ends of the top dowel have been fitted with screws which have been inserted into inch-long slots in the side boards and fastened with butterfly taps, as in Figure 14-3. Thus, when the taps are loosened, the dowels can be slipped down an inch (the length of the slots), which loosens the weaving in order to pull it forward.

If smaller articles are to be made, more screw holes can be bored along the sides of the frame to adjust the lower rod. Place mats and small rugs can be woven on this loom merely by raising the lower rod to the desired height, remembering always to allow for warp ends to be tied at the finish. The space between the sides needs no adjusting, for the width of the mat is determined by the number of warp strands strung on it.

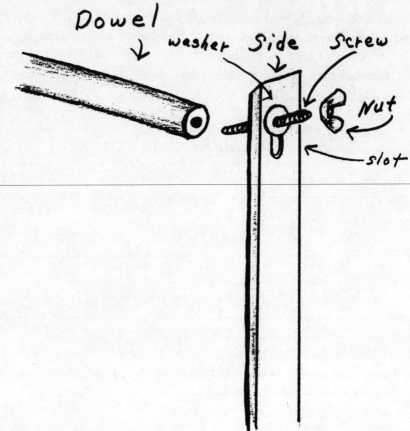

Fig. 14-3. *Ray made the large loom on which our cattail hammock was made in this manner, assembling the parts with nuts and screws.*

Tree Limb Loom

As we have said, looms for the weaving of wild materials can be as intricate as the most complicated of manufactured ones or as primitively crude as the materials themselves; it's your prerogative.

We are not going to discuss the intricate operation of the "boughten" looms, though the subject is fascinating; we'll leave that to cloth-weaving masters, and will instead describe some of the "fun" looms we have used, that can be manufactured by your own two hands from whatever old Mom Nature offers.

One of the simplest of these is the tree limb loom, shown in Figure 14-4. Simply find a tree that has a horizontal limb, not too far up for easy reach, and call this the top of the loom. Cut another strong stick, a few inches longer than the width of the article you are going to weave, and tie it to the limb with cordage, allowing it to dangle several inches longer than the desired length. This is, of course, to allow cord for tying the finished article.

You now have a gadget that looks like a swing, but no swinging; we're far too busy.

Now anchor the lower stick firmly by tying cords to it and then tying the cords to stakes which have been driven into the ground on a slant. The loom is now ready for the warp.

Tie the warp strands onto the tree limb and the bottom stick, about

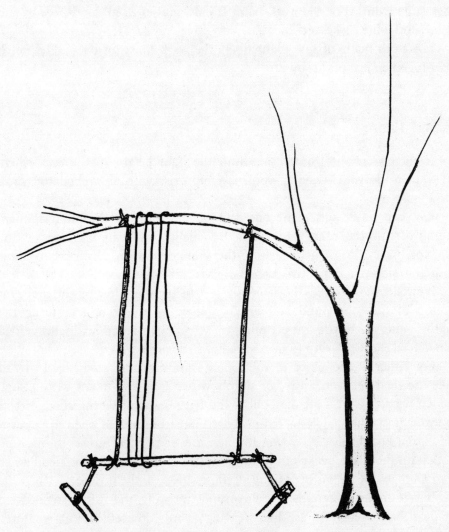

Fig. 14-4. Want to weave when you are out in the wilds? Try a tree limb loom.

171

one inch apart (depending on the type of article you are weaving). For a strip of weaving twice as long as the loom, wrap the warp around both the back and front of the loom. Then, after weaving one side, loosen the guy ropes of the stakes and pull the weaving over the limb to bring the unwoven side to the front for weaving. Now tighten the guy ropes and continue weaving.

If you are making a large item such as a hammock or floor or wall mat, the warp may be as much as two inches apart. For smaller items, especially when using grass for the weft, an inch or less is better.

Sisal or jute cord or even twine works well for the warp of this and other large looms. For the weft, palm fronds, grasses of all kinds, reeds, and cattails and other rushes are fine.

For cloth made of fine plant fibers the warp must, of course, be much closer together; just play it by ear.

Arched Loom

If there is no horizontal tree limb the right height in the area where you want to do your weaving, you may improvise with an arched tree limb as in Figure 14-5.

Dig two holes and plant one end of the limb in the ground; then, arching it, sink the other end. Then tie smaller limbs to the sides of the arch, for braces. Prop them against the ground in such a way as to allow the arch to slope back slightly.

Now tie another stick horizontally just below the curve of the arch, for the top of the loom; and still another stick lower down, measuring the length of the article you are planning to weave, with about six inches added (you'll need the extra warp to tie off the finished ends).

For either of the above looms you can use a heddle (see Fig. 14-1) to make the shed between warps, or simply weave over and under with a large wooden needle if the weft material is the type that can be threaded. If you are using grass, the heddle or batten board must be used to open up a shed. The batten board must be woven through the warp, then turned to one side to open up the space between the strands. This is slower than the heddle but does eliminate the necessity of tying all those strings to the heddle.

If you are using cattails or palm fronds for weft, the stiff base ends are usually strong enough to use like weaving swords or needles. But whatever you use, the weft must be pressed down tight after every row of weaving.

172

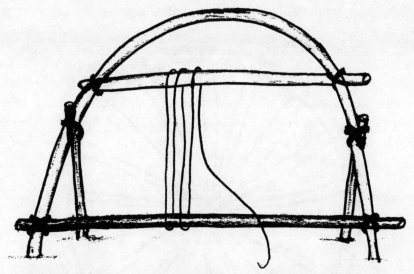

Fig. 14-5. *Even an arched limb, seated in the ground, can serve as a loom.*

Another loom we have seen, but never used, is one that is made in the same manner as that of the horizontal tree limb style, but instead of being anchored with stakes and guy ropes, is weighted by tying a couple of large rocks to the bottom stick.

Small Round Loom

A smaller loom for round items such as mats and hot pads can be made by tying a pliable stick into a hoop, wrapping the warp wagon wheel style around it (see Fig. 14-6), and, starting in the middle, weaving the weft in a tight circle over and under, alternating with each row, until the wheel has been filled with weft to the hoop.

Cut the limb hoop in several places and pull the pieces from the loops of weaving. The top hot pad in Figure 7-12 was made in this manner.

Hand Lift Sling Loom

This is a very practical loom which can be made entirely of materials to be found in the woods. The construction of it solves the heddle and shed problem in a unique way.

A small loom of this type is shown in Figure 14-7. This example can only hold a mat about twenty inches long, but we have made and used

173

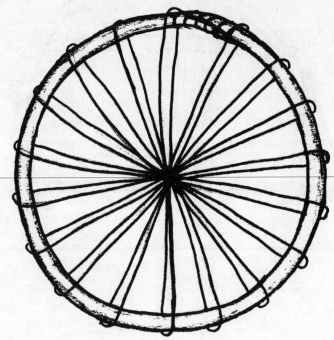

Fig. 14-6. A pliable limb, such as a willow whip, makes a round loom.

looms of this type large enough to weave mats three feet wide and six feet long to use as walls for a shelter.

First a strong sling-stick, several inches longer than the width of the item to be made, is tied hammock-style to a tree. On it are tied an uneven number of warp strands.

For this small mat, which is about fifteen inches wide, we first tied on five strands; for a larger one, increase the number accordingly.

Now drive five stakes into the ground, at a distance from the sling-stick that is several inches longer than you want the mat to be, for you will need extra length of cord at the ends for tying off.

Stretch the five warp strands taut and tie them to the stakes. Now tie four more warp strands on the sling-stick between those that are already on it. These four must be much longer than the five, for the weaving will take up some of their length. A good rule to follow is to make them at least a fourth longer.

Now tie the ends of the four warp strands to a lift-stick the same length as that of the sling-stick at the top. The loom is now ready for weaving.

Fig. 14-7. *One of the many kinds of looms that can be made of all wild materials is the sling loom pictured here. Notice how the warp can be lowered and raised to permit sheafs of grass to be laid across it. A large loom of this type was used for the grass wall panel described in Chapter 8 (see Fig. 8-8).*

To weave, raise the lift-stick and press several blades of grass up between the warp strands. Then lower the lift-stick to the ground, making another shed in which to place another row of grass (or cattails, or fronds).

Continue weaving in this manner, tamping the grass up tight each time with a stick or your fingers, until you have almost reached the stakes.

If the article you are weaving is one that must be strong, such as a hammock, weave warp cords across with the grass at several points, and tie them to the side cords. This will prevent the warp from spreading out as pressure is applied.

When the weaving is finished, take the mat from the loom and tie all the ends over the lift-stick. Leaving the sticks in the weaving is a good plan when the mat is to be used for a shelter wall or hammock; but if it is to be a floor mat, remove the sticks and tie off the ends of the warp in pairs to hold the weaving.

For a hammock, you will need end ropes with which to tie it up. A mesh of weaving that leads to a point works well for this.

Cut forty strands of warp, four feet long. Tie them between the warp on the two sticks. About four inches up, tie every two of these together in pairs. Then separate the pairs, and about four more inches up, tie them in pairs to those next to them, including the outside cords, which will not have a mate. Continue this tying until the fishnet type of mesh is in a point.

Now gather all the cords together, and braid them into a three-part braid to the end. You now have the rope with which to tie up the hammock.

Hunt up a couple of trees that are the right distance apart, tie up your hammock, and rest. You deserve it after all that work!

Picture Frame Loom

We've saved the simplest of all frames for the last. Just pure sneaky of us, for if we had given it first you would have used it and missed all the fun of experimenting with the others.

This one is a simple rectangle of four sticks, bound together at the ends, making the frame. Proceed to wrap on the warp as shown in Figure 14-8. Heddle and batten board can be used for this one, or over-and-under weaving, pressed down with the fingers.

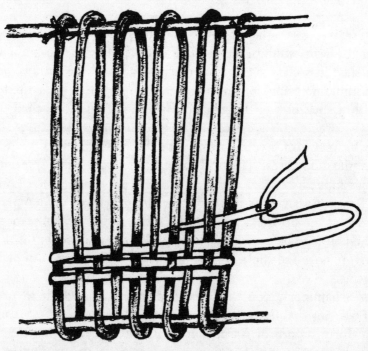

Fig. 14-8. *This drawing shows the detail of simple over-and-under weaving. The fingers, a needle, or a weaving sword can be used for this, depending on the size and closeness of the warp.*

CHAPTER 15

Dyes and Dyeing

From prehistoric times, the making of dyes has always been a big problem, for while one area will yield a plant or animal that will make a certain kind of dye, another will be lacking in that color. The dye makers of the different countries jealously guarded the materials and techniques used. So valuable, and difficult to obtain, were some of the colors (such as Tyrian purple, which was extracted from a certain shellfish) that they were reserved for the robes of royalty alone.

Trying to extract dyes from plant life is at once an exciting and frustrating thing. When a good, rich color results, you rejoice mightily, but when you have tramped the woods to gather certain leaves, roots, bark, and blossoms, follow all instructions for making dyes of them, and nothing happens except a slight tinge to the water—well!

After so much wasted effort, you may feel inclined to wash your hands of the whole thing and make a trip to the market for packaged dyes. These do work beautifully on most plant fibers, but aren't as much fun.

For those who do not have the time or desire to go gallavanting off into woods and fields we have included our findings on coloring plants with both wild and packaged dyes.

PACKAGED DYES

When using dyes purchased from stores, make the mixture a little richer for plant fibers than you would for wool or other cloth. You may follow the directions given for cloth, but boiling tends to weaken or crisp the plants and stronger dyes diminish the boiling time necessary.

Some plants take dye much faster than others. For example, sisal simply drinks it up, but glossy grasses, with their hard surfaces, are very reluctant to even take a sip and will require a longer time in the dye bath. But all in all, dyeing with the store-bought dyes is far more simple than making your own.

DYEING FROM NATURE'S MATERIALS

Being a proud member of that prestigious organization, the Outdoor Writers Association of America, and believing in its dedication to truth in reportage, I would feel that I was cheating if I did not give my readers the whole truth and nothing but the truth. For this reason it seems important that I discuss failures in my experiments as well as the successes.

Many writers feel that they can research from other writers' output, and (perhaps changing wording slightly in order to keep the old bugaboo "court suit" out of their hair) simply copy the experiences of others with all the appearance of authoritative knowledge. I too read everything on dyeing from wild materials that I could get my hands on, but then I plunged deep into the process of proving the writers' theories for myself. My kitchen went through a period when pans of elderberries, pokeberries, and sumac heads and bowls and bags of walnut leaves, crushed walnut hulls, stone-ground roots and bark and dozens of other odd specimens of plant life littered (and stained) cabinet, table, and range.

But I found out! *How* I found out! And believe me it was at times very discouraging. I came out of this crazy dyeing binge marveling that though one writer claimed that lily of the valley leaves will furnish a green to yellow dye, the ones I tried barely tinted the water. And following the instructions of another writer, who stated that corn shucks make a blue dye, I came up with a fine, pure quality of drinking water. I came to the conclusion that either those other writers had never tried these things and didn't know what they were talking about, or I was doing everything wrong.

178

Beige, tans, and light browns I produced in plenteous quantities, but despaired when striving for deeper, brighter colors.

And then late summer arrived and with it came the ripening of wild berries.

The first pan of elderberries plunged me into ecstasy, for from that one panful of juice came an unbelievably varied array of rich colors. There was deep (almost black) purple, bright purple, a luscious shade of magenta, orchid, lavender, and even light blue and a silvery gray-blue. It was amazing! And this experience made up for all the frustrations that preceded it.

The berries even dyed the difficult materials such as cattails and the glossy type of grasses, though of course these did not take the color as well or as evenly as sisal, jute, and other nonglossy materials.

Subsequent satisfying dyeing sprees produced other colors, but one I was not able to find in American plants was a pure deep blue. Evidently no one else had had any better luck at this, for other writers would invariably turn off the question of producing blue dye by suggesting that readers buy indigo at botanical shops. I was resigned to giving in and offering the same advice, until I discovered by accident a way to make blue dye from elderberries. (See the discussion of elderberries under the heading "Some of the Better Dye Plants," later in this chapter.)

This chapter will discuss primarily dyes that one can actually gather and process out in the wilds, over a campfire if so desired.

Strangely, the dyeing quality of plants varies at different times of the year, but it would be impossible to state that in summer certain plants will produce such and such a color and in fall another, for weather conditions also have an effect on them. A dry or wet season may or may not be bad for certain colors of dye plants; a late freeze can also affect them.

It is simple, though time-consuming, to extract color from plants. Use an enameled or glass pan. If bark or roots are used, dry and pulverize them, soak them overnight if possible, cover with water, and simmer until the water is a deep color; then strain.

For leaves, twigs, onion skins, berries, and blossoms, simply cover them with water, simmer, and strain through a cloth or strong paper toweling. The use of a potato masher, after the berries or leaves have softened, is an aid in extracting the juice.

Now place the material to be dyed in the dye bath and allow it to simmer a few minutes until it is the desired color. The fibrous plants can take a lengthy bath in hot water but it is damaging to some plants. With these it is better to use packaged dyes which require only a dunking in the hot dye bath. Examples are the maize-and-indigo belt and headband pictured in Figs. 8-3 and 8-5. Afraid that the boiling necessary with the natural dyes we happened to have would tend to weaken or crisp the swamp grass, we dipped coils of the grass in hot baths of yellow and blue Rit, with excellent results.

Of course, as we have said before, aging and curing plants in certain ways can cause them either to retain or lose their natural colors, and in some cases change them. Light and sun, during curing, fades plants, but allowing them to cure in shade helps to retain the natural greens. An exception is the buckhorn weed, which turns a lovely red-brown in both sun and shade.

Plants vary in their ability to take dyes but will usually dye better with the packaged dyes. The glossy ones are, as a general rule, more difficult to dye than those that have a dull, dry look. Fibers, such as sisal and jute, always dye better and more uniformly than blades and leaves. Tree limbs, such as willow whips, are the most difficult of all.

Vegetable dye, such as that used to dye Easter eggs, does well on fibers, when vinegar is added, but barely tints glossy blades.

Some of the Better Dye Plants

Walnut Hulls and Leaves. Green or almost matured walnut hulls will make a satisfactory brown dye. Depending on the amount of water used, it can range from a light tan through rust to dark brown. Dry hulls (again depending on the amount of water used) will produce a near black and several shades of gray.

To make dye from either of these, pound the hulls from black walnuts, cover them with water, and soak for several hours. Then simmer for an hour or more over a low fire. Strain through a strong paper towel (we like the type that has threads through it) or a cloth.

While the dye is still hot, place the material to be dyed in it. If this does not produce as deep a color as you want, put the dye back on the fire and simmer until it does.

Try to avoid too much cooking, for plants such as grass, palm fronds, and cattails tend to become brittle after they are dry.

A bit of copperas, which can be purchased at some drug stores and botany shops, is a good mordant to set the color of walnut hulls. Use about

Fig. 15-1. *The mashed hulls of black walnuts dye beautiful and lasting shades ranging from deep chocolate brown to a greenish tan, depending on the amount of water used.*

a teaspoonful to a gallon of water. When the desired color is obtained, take the material from the bath, dissolve the copperas in it, and return the material to it for a few more minutes. Rinse the material.

Elderberries. Elderberries are a delight to work with, though caution must be exercised to keep them from staining everything they come in contact with—including you. Rubber gloves will keep your hands from turning a rich dark purple.

Pick the ripe berries. Strip them from the twigs into a glass or enameled pan, and, using about twice as much water as berries, simmer them for about half an hour. During this time, mashing the berries with a large spoon or potato masher, or even a wooden paddle, helps to extract the juice. Strain.

Put a sample of the material to be dyed in the bath, for the colors of this dye can vary in a surprising manner. Note the length of time it takes to obtain the shade you want. For most materials this rich dye will produce a

Fig. 15-2. Elderberries furnish some of the finest dyes. The colors range from a deep rich purple through magenta and orchid, and we even discovered (by accident) that they would yield shades of deep to light blue with the addition of soda.

very dark purple in about ten minutes or less. For lighter shades, such as magenta, leave the material in the bath less time. And for the much lighter orchid, thin the dye with more water and test until the right shade is obtained.

This experimenting is much of the fun of producing your own wild dyes. The orchid shade I produced by adding hot water to the richer dye was lovely. And at one point I felt like the classic brand of mad scientist, for one example came out a lavender and another a light blue—and I have no idea what I did to cause it!

We were advised by a dear lady, who lived among the Indians of the West, to use a "handful of salt" to set the elderberry dye. This we did, and our colors do seem to be holding up well.

Our biggest surprise in working with elderberries was our accidental discovery of a way to make a deep blue dye from them. Once when gathering elderberries, Ray and I overdid the quantity, and with those I did not need for dye, I made some scrumptious syrup. Elderberry syrup is, by the way, very much like the blueberry syrup served at pancake houses.

When finally I made some buttermilk pancakes, we used some of this luscious purple syrup, and the stuff turned a deep indigo blue!

We were enthralled at the phenomenon. Obviously some ingredient in those pancakes performed the miracle.

More experimenting—this time with the syrup—and, yes, it was the soda. Ordinary baking soda turns the purple juice of the elderberries to a rich blue. I can't tell you the proportions to use (it was too late in the season for us to get more berries for experiments), but I think it would work to simply add soda to the juice until you obtain the shade of blue you want, testing a bit of white paper toweling or cloth as you work.

And if your experiments result in more surprising discoveries, I would appreciate hearing about it. Of such as we are great inventors born.

Hickory Bark. We have been told that hickory bark will produce a "clear, bright yellow," but there are many kinds of hickory trees. We experimented with the bark of a pignut hickory and, though we did not get yellow dye from it, we managed to get nice shades of rust and rosy beige. However, we must take the word of others that some hickory bark will yield bright yellow, for writers in many publications have attested to this. We will eventually find the right variety of hickory, but since only the bark from a living tree is used, we have been reluctant to cut into one. This would almost certainly kill the tree. For this reason we will keep a watch for a tree that is crowded in among others and would not do well, or one that is to be removed.

Chip the rough outside bark away, and cut small pieces of the smooth inner bark. Soak these, if possible, overnight; then simmer the chips for an hour or so over a low flame. Strain and test a sample of the material to be colored. It took us about ten minutes of simmering to get the rosy beige.

This dye, too, may be set with copperas, but our beige and rust are holding up well without it.

Sumac Berries. Sumac berries, when matured and turning red, will yield a red dye. (A warning: don't fool around with the sumac which has white berries, for this one is poisonous to some people and can cause a painful rash very much like that of poison ivy.)

Strip the red berries from the twigs, cover with water, and simmer for about half an hour. Strain through paper toweling or cloth.

Put a sample of the material to be dyed in the bath for as long as it takes to obtain the desired color. For light shades of pink and coral, thin

Fig. 15-3.   Sumac heads furnish a rosy tan.

the dye with more water. You may set these colors with powdered alum or copperas (about a teaspoon to a gallon of water).

Pokeberries. Gathered before they are dead ripe, pokeberries will produce a brilliant scarlet. For deep purple, add some of the roots and stems to the dye bath along with the berries. Simmer and mash these for about thirty minutes and then proceed to strain and dye a sample to determine the time needed to attain the desired color.

This dye may be set with acid vinegar or salt (about a cupful to a gallon).

Ferns and Grasses. Some ferns and grasses will produce a green dye, but here too, there are many varieties and the intensity of the dye color is influenced by the area and climate in which they grow. Experimenting is the answer. Gather the ferns with the richest green color. Please do not pull them up, for with the roots left in place, cutting the tops will not, as a general rule, hurt their future growth.

Cut the ferns into small pieces . and, if possible, allow them to soak overnight. Add a little more water in the morning, for they will take up much of it, and simmer until the water is a good color (about half an hour). Proceed to strain and dye a sample, timing it until the right shade is reached. Remember that a large quantity of material added to the bath will take up more of the dye. For this reason, it is a good idea to make the sample color a little darker than you want.

Mullein Blossoms. These will produce a yellow-brown, but are often hard to find in quantity.

Cover these flowers with water and simmer for about fifteen minutes over a low fire; then strain and dye a test piece of the material, timing it to determine the minutes required to get the right shade. Now dye the material. Alum may be used to set this dye.

Other Dye Plants. Obviously, we cannot give in detail all the dyes and their processing, for nature furnishes so many. But as we have said before, the experimenting is half the fun; so go out there and scout out your own. One rule to follow (though not always holding true) is to pinch the plant and rub it between your fingers. If the juices dye your fingers, you can be certain there will be dye color.

Fig. 15-4.   Pokeberries make lovely shades of red and coral.

Here are a few of the many plants available for dyes:

sage	shades of mauve
coffee grounds	beige and brown
tea leaves	ecru
red onions	an excellent bright red
yellow onions	yellow
mustard seed	a bright yellow
bloodroot	a good red
butternut hulls	tan and light brown
peach leaves	yellow
dahlias	gold
wild plum bark and root	red-brown
dock	beige and tan
beets	red

Mordants include alum, chrome, tin, copperas, cream of tartar, salt, and vinegar.

CHAPTER 16

Varnish and Lacquer

Some articles made from wild material are intended for only short-time use, but many are attractive enough to keep. A discussion of ways to preserve and enhance the beauty of these follows.

Most of the basketry we have described will hold up well without a finish of any kind, but an application of varnish, lacquer, or other clear coating will stiffen and brighten them. Most any clear coating (spray or brush type) works well; such a coating is especially effective on articles that have retained a good color.

For an example: Sabal palm, cured in the shade, will stay a pleasing tint of light green, and if we coat articles of this, it is always with a clear substance so that the color will not be obscured. However, occasionally some item will fade a nondescript shade and, if you like, you can paint them or stain them a wood color.

The burden basket in Figure 7-2 was made of willow spokes and cattail weavers, and the weavers had not aged properly but had dried in a thickly massed pile; as a result, mold spots had appeared. Since the basket had turned out well and we wanted to keep it, and since the spots in no way hurt the quality of the basket, we gave it a coat of oak-stain varnish. The brushed-on coating made the basket much firmer and much more attractive.

The coconut hat in Figure 3-17 had been made of fronds that also had been improperly aged and were spotty; so we gave it a mahogany stain, followed by a spray coating of clear lacquer. This gave it almost the exact color as the items of coconut fronds that we had frozen and allowed to lie in the sun. Actually, this hat had been given that treatment when it was made, but no treatment will correct damaged fronds. In such cases, a cover-up is the answer.

Another example is the little hanging basket in Figure 4-7. This one was made of Sabal palm fronds that had been cured in sun and rain, and though they were not spotted or discolored, the basket did seem rather fragile. For this reason, we gave it a spray coat of lacquer for strengthening. It worked, for the basket is now three years old and still swinging.

These experiments proved that we can correct the faulty coloring and enhance the beauty of basketry with paint, varnish, or stain; with a clear substance we can brighten even the good colors. But if at all possible, we like to keep these materials their natural color. This can only be done by choosing materials that are not bruised or old and by proper curing, as described in Chapter 2 of this book.

Index

(*Note:* Page numbers in italics refer to illustrations.)

189

Index

Index

Looms, 165, 166
    arched, 172, 173
    equipment, 167, 168, 169, 170
    hand-lift, 173
    large wooden, 92
    limb, 171
    picture frame, 176
    sling, 175
    small round, 173, 174
    tree, 170, 171

M

Maguey (*See* Agave)
Mats, 79

N

Napkin holders, 130
Needles (wooden), 21, 112

O

Onions (for dye), 186
Orange dye, 183, 186
Orchid dye, 181, 182, 186

P

Palmetto, 28
    fan, 75, 76, 77
    fly swatter, 77
    preparation and curing, 23, 24, 25, 26
Palms (*See* Cabbage palm, Coconut palm, *and* Palmetto)
Pin cushion (*See under* Pine needles)
Pine needles, 36
    bag, 127, 128, 129, 131, 132
    basketry, 131, 133, 134, 135, 136, 137
    gathering and curing, 23, 24, 34, 35, 36, 127
    napkin holder, 130
    pin cushion, 131
Pocket (leather), 163
Pokeberries (for dye), 185
Purple dye, 182

R

Raffia, 39
Red dye, 184
Reeds, 23, 24, 32, 33, 34
Ring weaving, 16, 17, 109
Rope making, 34, 35

S

Sabal palm (*See* Cabbage palm)
Sandals, 79, 80, 81, 82, 83
Shelter, 7
Shuttle, 90
Simple coil pattern, 19
Sisal (*See under* Agave)
Splicing, 99
Split weaving, 36, 37, 38, 138, 139, 140, 141, 142, 143, 144, 145, 146
Spokes, 13, 14
Sumac (for dye), 184

T

Thatched shelter, 57, 58, 59
Tree bark (*See* Bark)
Twined weaving pattern, 22, 67, 114, 115